IMAGES
of America

SLIDELL

For travelers, water towers signify an approaching town. Some, like Slidell's, tell a story. The bricks under the camellia represent the contribution of the brick industry in Slidell's early development. The boat on the water signifies fishing, shrimping, sailing, and recreational water sports. The tall pines represent the land and forest, filled with rich ozone air. The railroad tracks intersecting with a camellia represent the early development of Olde Towne. The camellia symbolizes the people's appreciation of the natural beauty in the area. (Courtesy of Trentis White.)

ON THE COVER: The waters of Lake Pontchartrain feed Slidell's bayous. Bayou Liberty branches off into Bayou Bonfouca, which winds its way into the heart of the city. The brackish waters of the bayou make it a great fishing hole. These unidentified young people are taking advantage of the occasion. (Courtesy of Slidell Museum.)

IMAGES
of America

SLIDELL

Arriollia "Bonnie" Vanney

ARCADIA
PUBLISHING

Published by Arcadia Publishing
Charleston, South Carolina

Library of Congress Control Number: 2014933963

For all general information, please contact Arcadia Publishing:
Telephone 843-853-2070
Fax 843-853-0044
E-mail sales@arcadiapublishing.com
For customer service and orders:
Toll-Free 1-888-313-2665

Visit us on the Internet at www.arcadiapublishing.com

*To my granddaughters Victoria and Alexandra, always keep a
place in your heart for history; and my best girl "Sweetie"*

CONTENTS

ACKNOWLEDGMENTS

Many thanks to Mary Ann Carollo, Alex Carollo, Slidell Cultural and Public Affairs, Brian Smith, Slidell Museum, Guardians of Slidell History, especially Willie Mae Pittman, and to all the families that contributed to the contents of this book.

INTRODUCTION

In 1699, when Jean-Baptiste Le Moyne, Sieur de Bienville, and Pierre Le Moyne de Iberville were exploring Lake Pontchartrain, very little attention was paid to the rich land north of the lake. It is only noted that on March 28, 1699, Iberville camped on a site described as a treeless, grassy point southwest of Slidell, thought to be Goose Point in Lake Pontchartrain.

Only the Acolapissa and Choctaw Indians were enjoying the rich resources of the area. An abundance of wildlife, natural food sources, rich soil for growing crops, and the variety of seafood supplied by the lake, bayous, and river were all that was needed. The Indians supplied New Orleans with a large amount of meat, fish, fruits, and vegetables on a daily basis. Schooners sailed across Lake Pontchartrain on a regular basis, with French settlements developing on all the major bayous and river basins. In 1725, Pierre Brou, the first permanent white resident in the parish, settled near the junction of Bayou Liberty and Bayou Paquet, trading with the local Acolapissa and, later, the Choctaw for meat and other food supplies.

In 1737, Francois Rillieux and his wife, Marie Marguerite Chenet, settled on Bayou Bonfouca with their son Vincent (for which Bayou Vincent is named) and another son who died at an early age. Francois died in 1760. The next year, his widow purchased the land between Bayou Bonfouca and Pearl River, which extended northward from Lake Pontchartrain to the bayou, from the Biloxi Indian tribe. The property included a large farm on Pearl River, which Vincent managed after his father's death, along with properties in New Orleans. He ran a shipping business across the lake, selling cattle from their farm and manufacturing tar and pitch, popular products in St. Tammany Parish. Vincent died on February 10, 1800. Rillieux's claim to the land was not recognized after the United States assumed control of Louisiana; however, portions of the large tract had already been sold.

John Guzman inherited one portion on the eastern side of Bayou Bonfouca from Barthlemy Martin in the early 1800s. In 1812, Congress organized a land district out of the Florida Parishes. All areas west of the Pearl River were considered in the Greensburg District, but there were no provisions made for surveying the private claims and public land in the area. On March 3, 1819, Congress officially named the region St. Helena District and provided for the survey. This process was called Americanization. Everyone was to apply for American patents to their land. Guzman was one of the individuals who applied to Congress, for his claim to tract 44 (5,500 acres) in St. Tammany Parish, which would eventually include the town of Slidell, south side Slidell, and Eden Isles to Lake Pontchartrain. Congress approved his claim on April 20, 1854. The family settled on a plantation on Bayou Bonfouca, Guzman owned a brickyard, ferry service, store, and hospital, located where Bayou Liberty Road crosses Bayou Bonfouca.

The Louisiana Purchase was signed on April 30, 1803. During that year, 314 sailing boats left the Port of Bayou St. John bound for Slidell and other ports in St. Tammany. Captain Martin and Pierre Robert made numerous trips to Bayou Bonfouca. Robert owned the land just north of the Guzman property. At Robert's Landing, he operated two docks on his property near the present depot, one for schooners and one for light boats. He had a supply house with boating and marine supplies, a general store, a ferry service, a sawmill, a brick plant, and a tar mill, along with horses and cattle he traded.

In 1806, shipbuilding along the bayous was beginning to take hold; the boatyard began catering to lake trade. Bayou St. John Lighthouse authorized 18 schooners carrying bricks from the north shore to New Orleans. There were 50 schooners built; 17 were built on the bayou between 1811 and 1840, along with the first steam-operated vessel.

Slidell did not escape the Civil War. Its ports were targets of a number of skirmishes. After Louisiana seceded from the Union and joined the Confederate States of America, the St. Tammany Regiment of Louisiana Militia, CSA, was organized under the command of Col. George Penn. In 1862, the Confederate gunboat *Corypheus* was captured while moored in Bayou Bonfouca. Union troops destroyed the lighthouse at the entrance of the bayou, and a skirmish took place between US troops and a scouting party of Partisan Rangers. The following year, Confederate troops captured and burned the barge *Helena* and schooner *Sarah Bladen* in the bayou. Both craft were smuggling wood and spars to New Orleans and bricks to Ship Island. Vessels moored in Bayou Bonfouca and Bayou Vincent was checked regularly for goods being smuggled from the north shore.

In 1875, Slidell was becoming the industrial capital of the South. Every day, 18 schooners carrying building materials to New Orleans left Slidell ports. Timber and cattle were a large source of income for many families that settled along the banks of the Pearl River, Bayou Bonfouca, Bayou Liberty, and Bayou Vincent.

In 1881, a small party of surveyors from the New Orleans & Northeastern Railroad began to break through neighboring forest, swamp, and marshes for another route toward Jackson, Mississippi. Finding high ground and available water transportation, their preliminary survey was completed. A 70-acre site was established in May for the headquarters, workmen quarters, and a plant at Robert's Landing, also known as Robert's Brick House.

In early 1882, a creosote plant was completed on Bayou Vincent for treating lumber to construct the railroad. Hotels and boardinghouses sprang up. Workers were brought in by the railroad to operate the plant. The engineer, foreman, and crews stayed for three years. Business was generated from sales of food, clothing, and large quantities of whiskey. There were a number of sawmills already established before Salmen, Hamlet, Bliss, and Elliot came to Slidell. The first telegraph line was installed connecting the north shore station to New Orleans and Meridian, Mississippi. By this time, 40 miles of track were laid, the bridge across Lake Pontchartrain was partially completed, and tracks were being laid to the lakeshore from Slidell.

In 1883, railroad engineers Bouscaren and Fremaux laid out the townsite. A wooden passenger depot was constructed on the west side of the tracks between Main and Pennsylvania. The first passenger train made its trip from Meridian to New Orleans on October 15, 1883. Baron Frederic Emile von d'Erlanger, one of the financiers, inspected the railroad on the first train out of New Orleans. He named the first stop north of Lake Pontchartrain Slidell Station in honor of his father-in-law, John Slidell, who was deceased by the time the railroad was completed in September.

On September 17, 1888, the first meeting of the Town of Slidell was held. A newly elected mayor, Seth H. Decker, and aldermen F. Salmen along with A. Provost, Oscar L. Dittmar, H. Maudin, and C.F. McMahon wrote and approved a charter for the town of Slidell. Sections 1 thru 13 were signed at the November 13 meeting incorporating the town and recorded in Covington, Louisiana, on March 7, 1893. When the charter was written, the town had a population of 200, and it comprised 2,320 acres.

One

SLIDELL STATION

On January 7, 1884, the Slidell Station opened and began receiving mail at its newly established post office in the station. Jacob Huff was appointed the first postmaster. A telephone line into the station made its first call on July 7, 1884; the call was between John Guzman of Slidell and General George Moorman of Mandeville, Louisiana. That same year, the New Orleans & Northeastern line reported revenue of half a million dollars. Its assets included 30 locomotives, 16 passenger cars, and 1,606 freight cars. The freight cars were mainly used to service the 55 sawmills between Meridian, Mississippi, and Slidell.

By 1910, the original depot was in deplorable condition. The mayor and aldermen sent a letter to the railroad to either replace or repair the old station. A proposed station was to be located between Bouscaren and Cousin Streets on the railroad right-of-way. However, this location was rejected. A second depot was built on the west side of the railroad tracks between Main (Maine) and Pennsylvania Avenues. This was a logical spot, since the line from Slidell to Lacombe, Louisiana, was operating, and Salmen Brothers was constructing the line from Slidell to Mandeville, Louisiana, at that same location. In 1913, a new depot was constructed in its present location. All around the station, hotels, stores, and saloons started popping up to accommodate the passengers.

On December 29, 1916, Emile Erlanger and Company sold its stock in the New Orleans & Northeastern line. At that time, the railroad became a member of the Southern Railway System. In 1996, Norfolk Southern Railroad donated the depot to Slidell. It was renovated with a grant obtained from the Louisiana Department of Transportation and Development, with funds received under the Intermodal Surface Transportation Enhancement Act of 1991 to renovate, preserve, and operate the depot. The depot was added to the National Register of Historic Places in 1996 as the New Orleans and Northeastern–New Orleans Greater Northern Railroad Depot.

The Crescent was the daily train service through Slidell in 2011. It showed revenues of $557,082 and total passengers of 7,316.

Slidell's first railroad station was built around 1882 and was located near Main (formerly Maine) and Pennsylvania Avenues. It housed the first post office and telephone line. Eventually, three rail lines would run through the heart of town. The railroad workforce is seen here at the station. (Courtesy of Slidell Museum.)

This second depot was built on the east side of the railroad tracks, between the Slidell-to-Lacombe line and the Slidell-to-Mandeville line. The beauty of Slidell's moss-covered oaks along the line can be seen here. Travelers boarding the train were destined for towns in Mississippi and points beyond. (Courtesy of GOSH.)

Before being torn down in 1912 to make way for a modern station, visitors and travelers arrived and departed this station daily. Travel to Slidell was by rail or schooner until ferry service began. (Courtesy of Mildred Pearce.)

The new depot was built in 1913, after the town's mayor and aldermen complained about the poor conditions of the previous station. It was constructed on the site of today's depot, between Teddy Street and Fremaux Avenue. All around the station, general stores, hotels, and saloons were built to accommodate newly arriving workers, travelers, and families settling in Slidell. (Courtesy of GOSH.)

The railroad workforce gathers around, and on, engine No. 429 in 1905. Seated at lower center are officials of the New Orleans & Northeastern Railroad. Chief engineer G. Bouscaren is in white shirt with dark tie. Next to him is general superintendent R. Carroll, followed by division engineer S. Whinnery and general freight agent H. Colbran. The railroad was the second-largest employer in town. (Courtesy of GOSH.)

Standing on one of the railroad's loading platform docks are four unidentified employees of Salmen Brick & Lumber Company. The company had its own sidetrack, railcars, and engines to move the lumber and bricks to the main line. (Courtesy of Slidell Museum.)

Early travel to and from Slidell was mainly by railroad. Standing on the platform waiting for the passenger train is Fritz Salmen (center) and his wife, Rosa Liddle Salmen. The small child and the others shown here are unidentified. (Courtesy of Slidell Museum.)

These unidentified gentlemen are part of the depot's workforce. The man fourth from left in a tie appears to be wearing a sidearm. He was possibly a railroad agent for the line. (Courtesy of Slidell Museum.)

This 1920s photograph shows a cattle car and two boxcars on the side of the train depot, waiting to be moved onto the main track. Boxcars were used along the train route as temporary housing for railroad workers. Many were used in areas where there was no town. (Courtesy of Mildred Pearce.)

The train has brought much prosperity and many travelers to Slidell over the years, but no freight was more heartbreaking than, in 2005, this endless line of FEMA trailers traveling through the city after Hurricane Katrina devastated the area. It became a daily sight for many months after the storm. (Courtesy of Bonnie Vanney.)

14

Two

TRAVELING TO THE NORTH SHORE

In the early 1800s, schooners and sailing vessels docked at Robert's Landing daily, bringing settlers and supplies. Train travel became a major part of the town's economy and growth through the early 20th century. Tourists came from all over to bathe in the pine rock water of the area's wells, believed to have healing powers.

As early as 1919, talk had begun on building a highway between New Orleans and Logtown, Mississippi, by way of Chef Menteur Highway, Rigolets Road, and Slidell. In 1926, the automobile brought new modes of travel. Ferry service from New Orleans to the north shore was a challenge. An excursion by car on poorly constructed gravel roads from New Orleans to Chef Menteur Pass ended by waiting in the hot sun and fighting off mosquitoes to cross the island and travel down Hospital Wall Road at the Rigolets Pass. Then, cars boarded another ferry, bound for the north shore, disembarking in 15 minutes onto a new, 300-foot landing pier at the end of Treasure Isle and motoring up Old Spanish Trail from the lake into town.

On February 18, 1928, the Watson-Williams Bridge (also known as the Robert S. Maestri Bridge and the Five-Mile Bridge) opened. The bridge was privately owned and imposed a toll of $1.25 per car. Gov. Huey P. Long opposed the idea of people paying to cross the lake, and he ordered the ferry services to be free and put into motion the construction of two free bridges. The Chef Pass Bridge opened in September 1929, and the Rigolets Pass Bridge opened in 1930. Slidell was the first stop for travelers after leaving New Orleans. Drivers and passengers could stretch their legs, get a cold drink, and play the slot machines at the White Kitchen on Front Street. The Triangle Service Station sold 50 to 100 cases of Coca-Cola on weekends and added more pumps to the station for customer convenience.

The city flag has three white stripes bordered with green, representing the three interstate highways that intersect in Slidell. The roadways and bridges are aspects of the infrastructure that have made Slidell an ideal place for businesses and industries.

This is one of many steamers built by the Canulette Shipbuilding Company on Bayou Bonfouca. The *Lake Saint Tammany* was launched in 1924. Piloted by Capt. Jim Howze and Frank Comfort, her daily route was across Lake Pontchartrain to New Orleans from Slidell and Mandeville. (Courtesy of Slidell Museum.)

On the waves for repair is the *Leta* of Pearlington, Mississippi. She appears to be getting an overhaul. A part of the Hursey Company ferry fleet, she was the fastest of the line. On a daily trip across the Rigolets, she could carry 12 cars and 50 passengers. On occasion, she would dock at the Pearlington ferry landing. (Courtesy of Slidell Museum.)

16

Ferry service from New Orleans to Slidell and other ports in St. Tammany began around 1919 and continued until the construction of the Chef Menteur and Rigolets Bridges. *Mollie Lee*, an independently owned ferry, was small compared to the Hursey Company's fleet of five ferries. (Courtesy of Slidell Museum.)

The *Hi-Way*, not the largest of the fleet, cost $50,000 to build. She had a capacity of 40 cars and 500 passengers and could cross the Rigolets Pass in 15 minutes. Her sister ferries were *Leta*, *Garibaldi*, *O.S.T.*, and *Hursey*. During the summer months, 2,500 cars crossed into St. Tammany Parish and traveled through Slidell. (Courtesy of Slidell Museum.)

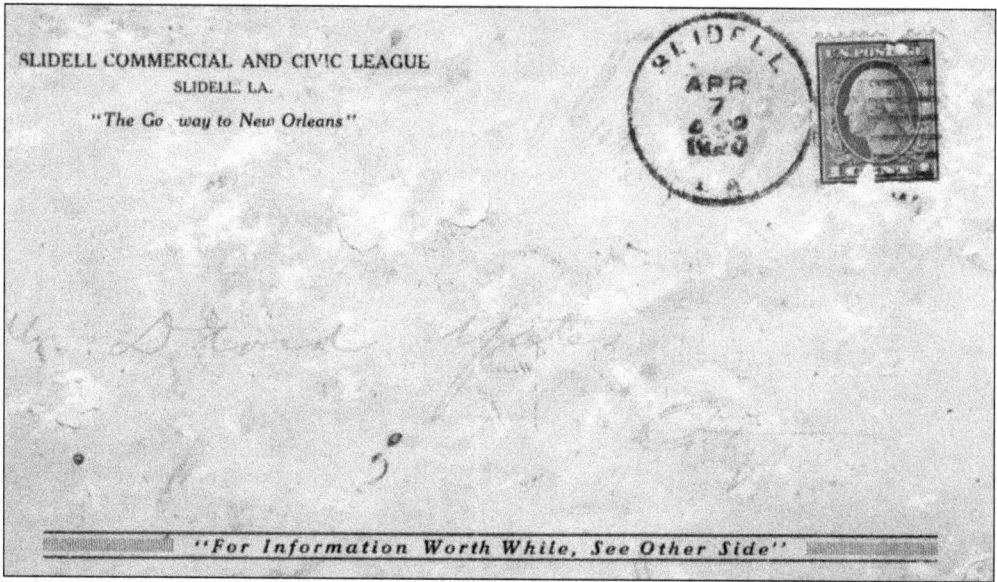

"For Information Worth While, See Other Side"

This postcard, addressed to David Yates, was sent by the Slidell Commercial and Civic League. Postmarked in Slidell and dated April 7, 1920, the card includes the motto "The Gateway to New Orleans." Unfortunately, little is know about the group. During this period in Slidell history, businesses were abundant and tourists were flocking to the north shore during the summer months to escape the heat and mosquitoes of New Orleans. Work was plentiful at the large sawmills, shipbuilding companies, and brick plants. Slidell's location in the heart of the Ozone Belt and its access to the healthiest water made it even more attractive. In Olde Towne, Sabrier's pavilion, a health resort and spa, stayed busy. (Both, courtesy of Slidell Museum.)

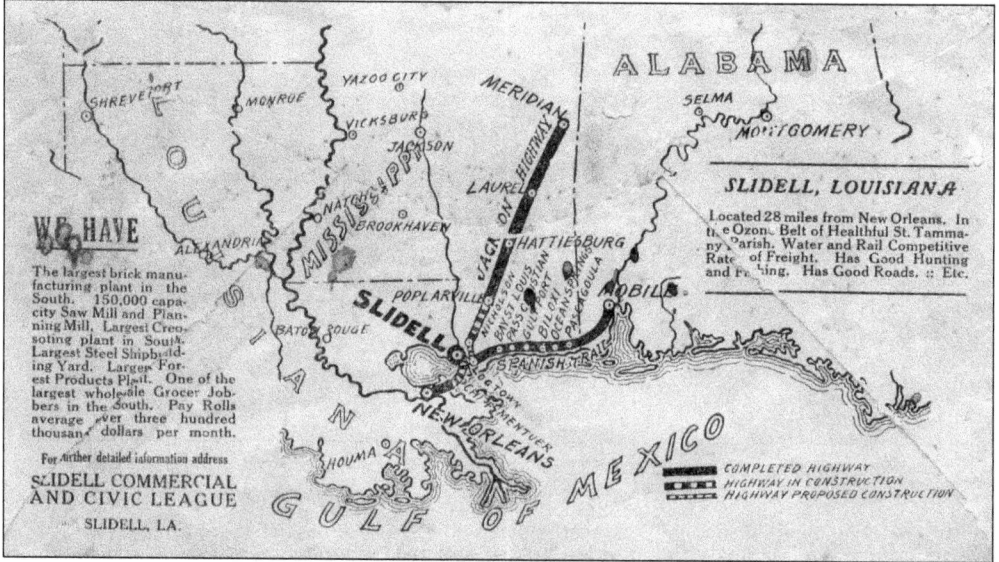

In 1926, the Louisiana Highway Commission hired the W. Horace Williams Company, an engineering firm, to explore the possibilities of building a bridge at Chef Menteur Pass and at Rigolets Pass. Slidell residents were hired for the construction project, including the unidentified workers in these photographs. Shown in the above photograph is one of the stationary Parker trusses, modified from Pratt trusses of 400 feet each. They were constructed from the St. Tammany side, and work proceeded toward the New Orleans East Land Bridge. Travel to the north shore became less complicated when, in 1928 and 1929, these two bridges opened. An average of one car every 10 minutes crossed the bridge. (Both, courtesy of Bonnie Vanney.)

The two bridges that connected the north shore to the south shore, ultimately eliminating ferry service, are the Rigolets Pass Bridge and the Watson-Williams (also known as Five-Mile) Bridge. Travelers on Highway 90 crossed the Rigolets Bridge. It was recently replaced with a high-rise bridge over the pass. (Courtesy of Bonnie Vanney.)

The Five-Mile Bridge, as it has come to be known, was heavily traveled before Interstate 10 was constructed in the 1960s. Opened in 1928, the bridge connected Slidell to New Orleans on Highway 11. It is used today by many residents living on the south end of Slidell. (Courtesy of Mildred Pearce.)

Built in the early 1920s, the Commercial Hotel was a grand building, located across the street from the town's present depot, on the south corner of Front Street and Fremaux Avenue. This two-story building was not only convenient to the train, but it was next door to the Neuhauser Bros. general merchandise store. The hotel offered free sample rooms to travelers and drummers (traveling salesmen). It was famous for its Bird Cage Saloon, operated by Mr. and Mrs. H.D. Varlie and, in later years, by Mr. and Mrs. S.H. Lott. To the left of the Commercial Hotel in the above photograph is Neuhauser Bros., followed by Spanish Gardens, a dining and dancing establishment. Baker's Saloon is at the far left. The 1920 postcard below offers a different look at the hotel. Visible in the foreground is the fence of the train depot. (Both, courtesy of GOSH.)

Commercial Hotel,   Slidell, La.

Jake B. Spence was from Mississippi. He moved to Louisiana when he took a position as a foreman of the Southern Railroad trestle maintenance crew, stationed at the south end of the trestle, until 1922. He moved to Slidell and opened a service station and café at 2859 Carey Street. Later, he built a two-story business and residence on the corner of Front Street and Pontchartrain Drive, Spence's Bar, better known as the Curve Inn. He sold the business to Nick Sansone, who operated it for 47 years. St. Christopher's Curve Inn closed in October 1987 after fire destroyed the landmark. The above photograph shows the original Curve Inn in 1930, with the family residence in the rear. Shown below is the last Curve Inn before it was destroyed. (Above, courtesy of Slidell Museum; below, courtesy of GOSH.)

Jake Spence took a few years off after selling the Curve Inn. In 1939, he decided to go back into business. He bought a larger parcel of land down from his previous location on Highway 11 and erected another two-story building with residence upstairs, calling it Spence's Café. He operated the business until 1943, when he sold the thriving business to Sam and Elizabeth Bosco. It was remodeled and opened as Bosco's Restaurant and Bar, pictured above. The motel seen below was added to the side, as well as a large room that could be partitioned for meetings, dances, and parties. Local bands played on weekends and for special occasions. (Both, courtesy of Slidell Museum.)

Pictured is one of the bands that played at Bosco's on a regular basis in the 1940s. The members are, from left to right, Joe Blackman (piano), Hal Gilda (leader and bass), Sparky Penton (drums), Elmer Fortier (vocals and tenor saxophone), Jack Galatas (trumpet), Oscar Davis (alto saxophone and clarinet), and Ralph Rousseaux (alto saxophone). (Courtesy of GOSH.)

The Curve Inn was famous for its delicious fried chicken. Many residents and travelers ate Sunday dinner at the restaurant. Local businessmen were part of the lunch crowd during the week. Jake Spence is pictured here behind the bar in 1937. (Courtesy of Slidell Museum.)

The Fontainebleau Hotel Court was one of many small motor courts built in the 1940s. The main highways coming into Slidell are Highway 90 and Highway 11. Accommodating the weary traveler were seven to ten cottages with kitchenettes and drive-in carports. Rates per night ranged from $1 to $2, depending on the number of beds per unit. This hotel had a swimming pool for the customers' pleasure. The Fontainebleau was located on the corner of Front Street and Gause Boulevard. At night, its lighted sign boasted air-conditioning. Gause Boulevard was a single-lane dirt road. Private homes can be seen in the background to the right in the above photograph. (Both, courtesy of Slidell Museum.)

One of Slidell's most famous landmarks was the White Kitchen, built in 1931 on Front Street. Onesine Faciane had a humble beginning in 1926, opening a hamburger and sandwich shop on Front Street. The forerunner to the White Kitchen chain was White Kitchen Cellar. After becoming successful in the business, Faciane changed the name to White Kitchen, perfecting open-flame barbeque and a secret sauce. It is said that his famous sauce was a gift from the Bowden family when they closed their barbeque business, located down the block from him. He added a logo of an Indian kneeling at a campfire. This logo was displayed at his three locations: two in Slidell and one in New Orleans. He continued to expand the business and added a bus stop for the Bayou Bus route, which ran between Bayou Liberty, Covington, and Slidell. The full-service station was open 24 hours a day. This aerial photograph, taken in the mid-1930s, shows the White Kitchen on Front Street; it is the large two-story building in the center of the photograph. Other structures that can be seen down Robert Street, the road intersecting with Front Street left of center, include Poole's Funeral Home, the third building on the right side of the street, just above the center of the image. The two-story building directly across Robert Street from the funeral home was the Community House. The first two-story building on Front Street from the left is Bank of Slidell, and the two-story building to the bank's left is the Slidell Masonic Lodge 311. (Courtesy of GOSH.)

Most anyone traveling through Slidell in the 1930s, 1940s, and 1950s stopped at the White Kitchen. It might have been for the food, the legal whiskey, or the gambling. The parking lot was always full. Carhops served customers on the weekend. It was a great place to take a date. Taxi service was available for residents, and gentlemen met at the barbershop for the local news. This photograph is of the White Kitchen on Highway 90. (Courtesy of GOSH.)

The White Kitchen was the center of community activity. In 1951, a 25th-anniversary celebration brought people from Mississippi and New Orleans to celebrate the event. A beauty contest was held, and decorated cars lined the parking lot. Miss White Kitchen was crowned before the crowd. (Courtesy of GOSH.)

white kitchen specialties

Indian Style Barbecue Dinner
Served With French Fried Potatoes, Vegetable,
Salad, Butter, Hot Biscuits.
1.35

Reg. U. S. Pat. Off.
Est. 1926

FROM THE
GROETCHEN ROTARY COOKER

Choice Western Sirloin Steak........................
Sizzling Hot, With Fried Onion Rings, French Fried
Potatoes, Salad, Butter, Hot Biscuits.

Choice Western T-Bone Steak........................
Sizzling Hot, With Fried Onion Rings, French Fried
Potatoes, Salad, Butter, Hot Biscuits.

Choice Filet Mignon........................
Sizzling Hot, With Fried Onion Rings, French Fried
Potatoes, Salad, Butter, Hot Biscuits.

Seasoned Hamburger Steak........................1.00
With French Fried Potatoes, Salad, Butter, Hot Biscuits.

Sizzling Western Pork Chops Lunch........................1.25
With French Fried Potatoes, Salad, Butter, Hot Biscuits.

White Kitchen Special Chicken Dinner........................1.35
(Broiled or Fried)
With French Fried Potatoes, Salad, Butter, Hot Biscuits.

Choice Breaded Veal Cutlet........................
With Mashed Potatoes, Vegetable, Salad, Butter, Hot
Biscuits.

Pan Fried Calf Liver........................1.35
With Smothered Onions, Potatoes, Vegetable, Salad,
Butter, Hot Biscuits.

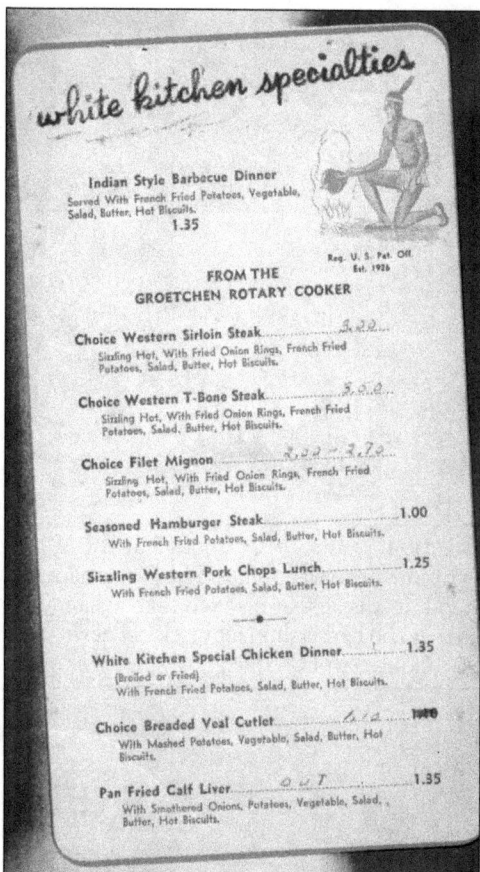

These are two pages of a 1950 foldout menu from the White Kitchen Restaurant and Bar. A variety of food was listed on the menu. At the top right corner of the photograph to the left is the famous Indian logo. Prices were reasonable for the times. Beverages ranged from coffee (5¢) to bottle beer (30¢). The most expensive were malted milk and milk shakes. Inside the menu was an advertisement for the two party and banquet rooms available for special events. The Mirror Room was in Slidell, and the Rose Room was on Highway 90 and Short Cut Road. (Both, courtesy of Slidell Museum.)

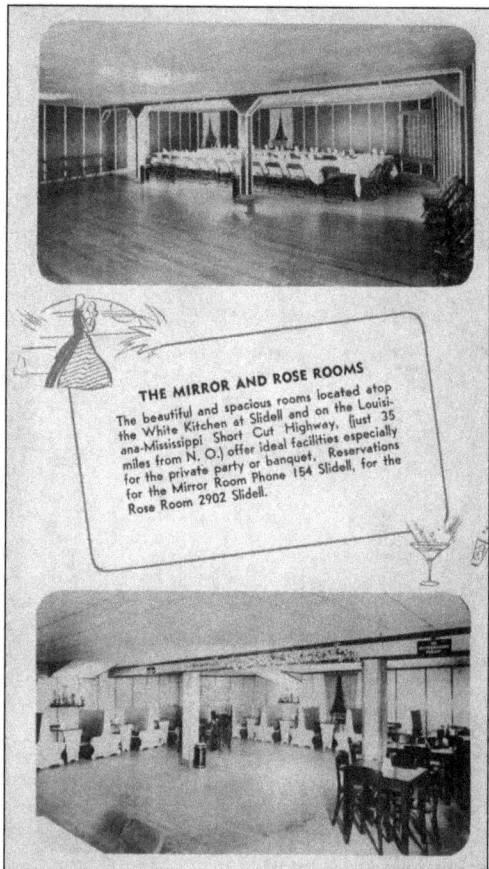

THE MIRROR AND ROSE ROOMS
The beautiful and spacious rooms located atop the White Kitchen at Slidell and on the Louisiana-Mississippi Short Cut Highway, (just 35 miles from N. O.) offer ideal facilities especially for the private party or banquet. Reservations for the Mirror Room Phone 154 Slidell, for the Rose Room 2902 Slidell.

Three

BOATS, BRICKS, AND BOARDS

Slidell's industry was the backbone of its economy, even before the railroad was completed. Departures and arrivals of schooners leaving Slidell ports bound for New Orleans kept hundreds of men working. Tar, pitch, turpentine, rosin, charcoal, lime, timber, bricks, sand, wood products, wool, fleece, and even silk were being exported.

Salmen Brick & Lumber Company built Salmen Town, an eight-block-square area north of Bayou Patassat to house its employees. A total of one million bricks were shipped to New Orleans for construction of the St. Charles Hotel and the *Times-Picayune* building on Camp Street. New Orleans ordered 23 million bricks for building its sewer and drainage system. Other brickyards began production soon after Salmen, including Slidell Brick & Tile Company and a more notable one still operating today, St. Joe Brick Works.

Commercial shipbuilding began in 1880. Earlier, small yards produced schooners and sailing vessels of all lengths. Salmen's original shipyard was sold a number of times, until, in 1993, under Southern Shipbuilding, it closed for good. While in production, the yard built a ship as large as 229 feet, tugboats for the US Army, and net tenders for the US Navy during World War II.

Aside from the 55 sawmills reported along the railroad line from Slidell to Meridian, the creosote plant set up by the railroad was in full production. It was the largest in the country, producing crossties and pilings for bridges and railways. In 1970, the plant was disassembled; it was abandoned in 1986.

Textron Marine and Land System in Slidell, the one remaining industry, has a business office on Gause Boulevard and a working plant on Front Street. It produces armored personnel carriers. At one time, its building housed Bernard Lumber Company, which manufactured factory-engineered homes, a reminder of years past and the area's strong lumber industry.

This photograph shows part of Salmen Lumber Company's yard. The large sheds are for preparing and dressing timbers. The company had timber operations within 75 miles of Slidell. On the left is where the lumber was stored before being shipped to its destination. Salmen cut the canal, in the background, off of Bayou Boufouca. A barge loaded with logs can be seen on the canal. (Courtesy of Slidell Museum.)

Salmen Lumber Company covered 40 acres between Bayou Patassat and today's Bayou Liberty Road. The plant manufactured cypress lumber, yellow pine, round pilings, shingles, and laths. Laths were used in early years in houses to hold plaster to the walls. The sawmill had a production capacity of 60,000 feet daily; the planing mill produced 50,000 feet each day. (Courtesy of Slidell Museum.)

Because of the abundance of pines, one of the area's main exports was turpentine. Shown here is a cooperage in the middle of a pine forest. Here, barrels were made to store the turpentine for shipment. (Courtesy of GOSH.)

The buildings in this photograph are Salmen brick kilns. Here is where the bricks were fired and made ready for delivery. A total of six kilns and nine drying sheds were in this location of the plant. (Courtesy of GOSH.)

Salmen's lumberyard had three sets of tracks leading to different loading docks. One led to the dressed lumber shed, and the other two led to the planing mill and shingle mill. Here, unidentified workers stand on a loading dock for dressed timber and pilings. Workers hold tools used to handle the large pilings. (Courtesy of Slidell Museum.)

A Salmen-owned schooner on a return voyage from Nicaragua unloads at the dock on Bayou Bonfouca. Mahogany and other fine wood were harvested from Salmen-owned property overseas and brought to a special section of the plant for processing. (Courtesy of GOSH.)

This early-1900s photograph shows the massive amount of area the Salmen Brick & Lumber Company yard covered. The main New Orleans & Northeastern Railroad track is right of center. Emerging from the bottom of the photograph, two tracks split off into the plant, and a third rail line continues toward the back of the operation. The first set to the left of the main line went to the kilns and pressed brick storage shed. The next set went to the dry clay shed. The last went to the timber dock and loading platform. In order to move its products, Salmen owned 4 engines and 250 railcars. On the plant site was a machine shop, carpentry unit, sheet-metal shop, and blacksmith shop, along with a full-support foundry. The front part of the operation was the brickworks, and the back half was for timber processing. Salmen provided housing on the site for its employees. (Courtesy of GOSH.)

When the New Orleans & Northeastern Railroad began building the rail line to Slidell, crossing Lake Pontchartrain was not a challenge. It hired Flitcher, Wessenburg & Company from Chattanooga, Tennessee, to construct the train trestle. In order to build the 25 miles of trestle and its approaches, timber for the bridge had to be creosoted to protect it from the water. At an estimated cost of $1.25 million, 30 million feet of lumber was needed. The railroad company opened a creosote plant in 1881; completion of the project was required by November 1, 1882. Above, timber waits to be sent to the plant. The photograph below shows a larger timber being hauled individually. (Both, courtesy of GOSH.)

Pictured here is the New Orleans & Northeastern Railroad Company's creosote plant in 1888. The huge cylinders held millions of gallons of creosote. They were 100 feet in height and 6 feet in diameter, constructed of solid iron. The plant was located off present-day West Hall Avenue and Bayou Vincent. (Courtesy of GOSH.)

The creosote plant was sold in 1890 to businessmen from New Orleans, who changed the name to Southern Creosoting Company. Seen here is Gulf State Creosoting Company's pile driver. This firm bought the plant in 1923. This barge and equipment was used to drive the 90-foot pilings into the ground. (Courtesy of Slidell Museum.)

Salmen Brickyard was the largest manufacturer of clay products in the South. It produced a quarter of a million bricks daily and was equipped with the latest in machinery to handle the job. The company laid 12 miles of rail to move its products. Shown here is a rail-mounted power shovel. Unidentified employees man the equipment. (Courtesy of GOSH.)

Fritz and Albert Salmen built a vast empire in lumber and bricks. Along with timbers and pilings, they manufactured fine lumber used in many homes in New Orleans Uptown and Garden District. (Courtesy of GOSH.)

Salmen Shipyard on Bayou Bonfouca was renamed Slidell Shipbuilding Company in 1914. The Salmen brothers, along with Andrew D. Canulette, were the main stockholders. Here, a barge is under construction in the graving dock. When it is completed, water will be let in slowly to fill the area and equal the bayou level. Gates will be opened, and the barge floated out. (Courtesy of Slidell Museum.)

Under government supervision, Louisiana Shipbuilding Corporation's principal owners became the Canulette family. Under their management, this wooden freighter was launched in 1918. Shipyard workers can be seen standing on the dock, watching her slowly slide off the waves and into the water. On her stern, a Norwegian flag flies, indicating her port of call. (Courtesy of Slidell Museum.)

These two tug boats, built 19 years apart at Canulette Shipbuilders, show not only the progress of the industry, but also the continued growth of shipbuilding in Slidell. In the above photograph, the tugboat *Andrew* docks at one of New Orleans' many ports. Constructed in 1920, this wooden hull and cabin served her purpose in towing and docking ships into port. Shown below is the launching of the tugboat *A.D. Canulette* on Bayou Bonfouca in 1939. The all-steel fabricated hull and cabin reflect changing technology, from the planking and corking of 1920 to the welding and riveting of 1939. (Both, courtesy of Slidell Museum.)

Both of these ships were constructed at Louisiana Shipbuilding Corporation. The wooden cargo freighter in the photograph above was constructed of an all-steel frame, with wood planking applied to the hull. Approximately 200 feet long, her destination and port of call are unknown. The steamer *Maple*, pictured below, was christened in 1917. This 229-foot oceangoing ship was the largest wooden vessel afloat of her time. She was owned and operated by the Norwegian Shipping Lines. That same year, the company ordered and accepted delivery of four other steamers. Slidell's shipyard was known worldwide for its quality and dependability. (Both, courtesy of Slidell Museum.)

The Canulette brothers moved the shipbuilding company down Bayou Bonfouca from its original location in 1920 and changed its name to Canulette Shipbuilding Company. It would eventually become Southern Shipyard until it closed. During World War II, the shipyard employed 1,900 workers for the war effort. The above photograph shows the launching of a government-owned ship in 1943 on Bayou Bonfouca. Some of the yard workforce is on hand to watch. The shipyard was under contract with the Army to build tugboats and with the Navy to build 183-foot net tenders. Below, a Navy net tender is afloat in 1944, waiting for delivery. (Both, courtesy of Slidell Museum.)

The shipyard machine shop is a main part of a ship's construction. Here, propeller shafts, ruttier shafts, stern tubs, gears, and gearboxes are machined. In 1943, Canulette's machine shop stayed busy with construction of vessels commissioned by the government. Shown in the above photograph, next to the large lathe, is Harold Berrigan (right) machining a ruttier shaft. On the floor are two propeller shafts. Left is Robert Rugan, and in the far right is John Panks, standing by a horizontal boring mill. Below, Robert Rugan is on the horizontal mill, working a job. (Both, courtesy of Slidell Museum.)

The opening of the two bridges from New Orleans in the early 1920s encouraged people to buy land on the north shore. Even though industry was Slidell's backbone during the 1800s and 1900s, this brochure listed only one commercial piece of property. All the rest were residential and farmland; a number of pieces were listed as being on the scenic bayous. An interest in farmland was due to Oscar R. Brugier and his experimentation in the practical development of certain methods and use of undeveloped resources in the area. He showed the neglect of the rich soil for farming and proved that the possibilities were endless in the production of cotton, sugarcane, and strawberries. Even the raising of livestock and poultry could result in a productive market. (Courtesy of Slidell Museum.)

In 1891, the Schneider family acquired St. Joe Brick Works, located north of Slidell on the New Orleans & Northeastern Railroad line. It was established as a brickworks and a small community of 200 people, with two stores, one barroom, and a blacksmith shop. The company would later be named Schneider Brick & Tile Company. Shown seated at center is Pete Schneider. Surrounding him are, from left to right, Bernard, Claude, John, Matthew, and Henry. (Courtesy of Slidell Museum.)

The Schneider Brick baseball team was one of many company teams that were started in Slidell, playing ball against other local establishments at Salmen Field. Unfortunately, none of the players can be identified. (Courtesy of Slidell Museum.)

Textron Marine and Land Systems is Slidell's newest industry. It is housed on the site that was once Salmen Brick & Lumber, later Bernard Lumber Company, a manufacturer of prefabricated homes. At the Front Street plant, tactical armored patrol vehicles are manufactured. (Courtesy of Brian Smith.)

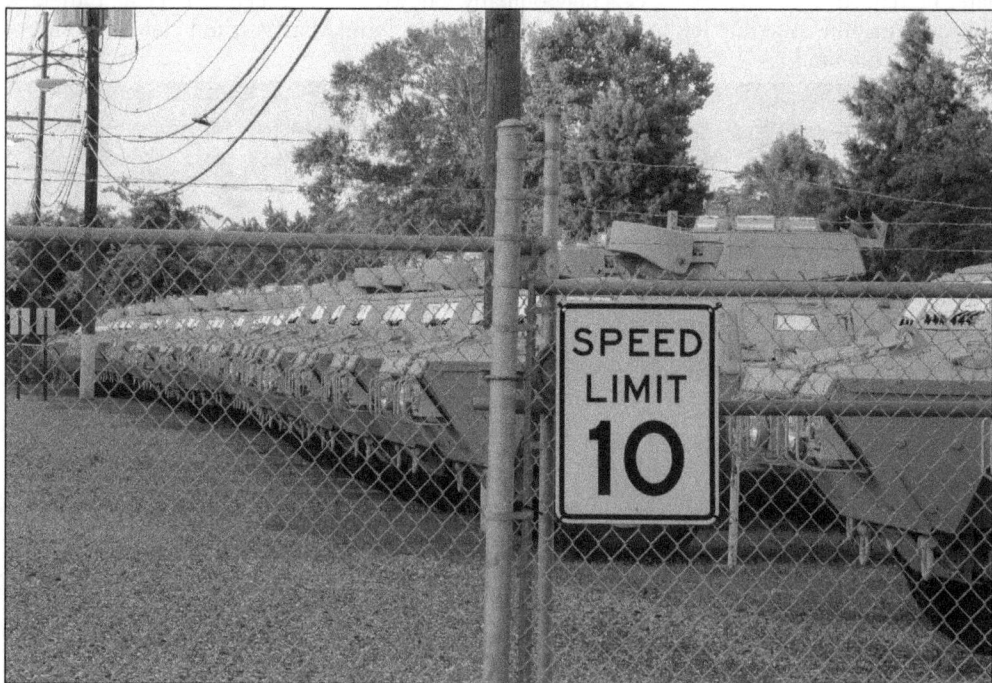

Textron occupies two locations in Slidell: one on Front Street and the other on Gause Boulevard. Shown here is a line of land vehicles waiting to be delivered. Textron is one of Slidell's largest employers. (Courtesy of Brian Smith.)

This aerial photograph shows the massive complex that launched Slidell into the race for space. The population went from under 5,000 to over 10,000 by 1970. Slidell is located between Stennis Space Center in Mississippi and the Michoud Assembly Facility in New Orleans East. (Courtesy of Slidell Museum.)

In 1962, the Slidell Computer Complex was opened on the corner of Gause Boulevard and Robert Road. Many families moved to Slidell, and many stayed after the complex closed. (Courtesy of Slidell Museum.)

Pictured here is one of the large computers that were housed at the Slidell complex. NASA closed the office in 1994 and later donated the building to the city. (Courtesy of Slidell Museum.)

Discovery flew the 100th space shuttle mission. It was launched on October 11, 2000, from Kennedy Space Center. The space program gave Slidell a great economic boost when it arrived in the 1960s. Many Slidell residents still work at the other two complexes. (Courtesy of GOSH.)

Four

OLDE TOWNE

As the town grew, it brought entrepreneurs who opened all types of businesses to cater to everyone's needs. The biggest interest was boardinghouses serving hot meals and saloons. In 1910, the town council issued eight permits at $500 each. As the town grew, so did its need for other retail business. Until the middle of the 20th century, the town was mainly centered on the old depot. Early development started with Slidell Ice and Light Company on the north end on Florida Avenue and Salmen Commissary on the south on Cleveland Street.

Along 12 blocks of Front Street were hotels, saloons, a blacksmith shop, stables housing a horse-and-buggy taxi service, a barbershop, fruit stands, a furniture store, a dry cleaners, a bank, a clothing store, and the largest merchandiser in St. Tammany Parish.

In 1920, the heart of town was centered on Dr. Polk's Drug Store (now Time Out Bar). Around the corner were Mrs. McDaniel's Store, Walter Abney Bakery, Levy's Meat Market and Grocery Store, and Sam Dimecilli's Fruit Stand. Around the other corner was Andrew Carollo's Store and Fruit Stand (now KY's). Across the street was G.A. Mire's Store. In the middle of the block was the Peter Lalumia Picture Show. Across the street were Champagne's Store and Pete Pravata's Candy Store. There was an open-air dome picture show operated by Josephine Jahraus behind the Bank of Slidell, Ben Giordano's Shoe Store, and Haas 5 and 10 Cents Store.

After a fire destroyed some of the buildings on Front Street across from the depot, the Neuhauser family erected a two-story building on the corner of Front Street and Fremaux Avenue. Small, independently owned businesses were opening on Front Street to Liddle Avenue (Pontchartrain Drive). The Pravata family occupied the triangle between Fremaux and Erlanger Avenues. J.B. Spence opened Spence's Service Station and Café on Carey Street. He later moved to the corner of Front Street and Pontchartrain Drive and opened Curve Inn. The famous White Kitchen was opened in 1926. The 1960s saw development in north Slidell and on Gause Boulevard.

Slidell's central business district now consists of quaint retail shops, antique stores, museums, restaurants, and bars—a very different landscape from years past.

The Salmen Commissary was opened in 1890 on the west side of the railroad tracks. Initially built of wood and painted white, it was replaced in 1893 by a brick building on the corner of Front and Cleveland Streets. In the early days, workers were paid partly in cash and partly in chits, which had to be redeemed at the commissary. (Courtesy of GOSH.)

This 1950 photograph is of an appliance store located on Front Street. The building has had a number of occupants over the last 63 years. Recently, it was home to a flooring company, and presently, it is occupied by a tire and hubcap dealer. (Courtesy of Mildred Pearce.)

Mrs. Evan's Boarding House is pictured here in 1905. Evans (first name unknown) also owned and operated the City Saloon. There were a number of boardinghouses in Slidell during the industrial boom. They housed not only workers, but also travelers and tourists during the summer months. (Courtesy of Slidell Museum.)

Mrs. Taylor's Boarding House, seen here in 1922, stood on the corner of Second and Erlanger Streets. It was within walking distance of the train depot. Established in 1913, the building was torn down in 1986. (Courtesy of GOSH.)

The above photograph shows one of Slidell's many saloons. Its location and the names of the individuals seen here are unknown. In a meeting in 1908, the town's council granted eight liquor licenses. During the 20th century, there were 13 saloons in the town. Liquor licenses cost $500 per establishment, and some owners had two and three saloons. In those days, saloons were segregated, and women were not allowed to enter or loiter around them. In 1907, the town council appointed a committee to instruct liquor dealers in how to keep women from hanging around their establishments. The below photograph is of an unknown saloon in Olde Towne. (Both, courtesy of Slidell Museum.)

Edgar Feliciine Perilloux moved to Slidell in 1890. He owned a number of properties and businesses in Slidell. He was a clerk to Slidell's mayor, aldermen, and city tax collector. The two-story brick building shown above was constructed in the early 1900s to compete with the Salmens' building on the other end of town. The Perilloux building, located across the street from the train depot, was later sold to Harry Hoyle, who opened a saloon and rooms to rent. Edgar Perilloux is standing on the right in the c. 1904 photograph. Another Perilloux business, a retail liquor outlet, was operated by his son. Seen below in 1905, the business was located on the corner of Front and Bouscaren Streets. (Both, courtesy of Slidell Museum.)

Cattle and other farm animals were free to graze all over town, but rich land to the south was their favorite location. William Rousseaux is seen here walking his cows down College Street to his dairy for milking. (Courtesy of Slidell Museum.)

Oxen teams were used to pull loads of logs to the processing plant. In this photograph, an unidentified driver pulls a wagon down Front Street. In the background is the Commercial Hotel. (Courtesy of GOSH.)

Mrs. M. McDaniel Millinery and Shoes was located on the southeast corner of Carey and Cousin Streets. The ladies and gentlemen in this photograph are unidentified. McDaniel's (first name unknown) store carried ladies' wear, hats, shoes, and other millinery items from New Orleans. The sign on the front of her building reads, "We sell Martinez Shoes, makers of the named Apex Shoes, New Orleans U.S.A." This building was replaced in 1917 by a two-story structure. (Courtesy of Slidell Museum.)

Levy's Meat Market and Grocery Store was located on the northwest corner of First and Cousin Streets. Solomon Levy and his wife had 10 children; their family living quarters was above the store. Pictured in front of his business in the early 1900s are Levy (right) and nine of his children. Recently, a fire destroyed this building in Olde Towne. (Courtesy of GOSH.)

Slidell had many mom and pop stores outside of town. This rural grocery store, owned by the Cousin family, was located on the left side of Highway 190 West. (Courtesy of Slidell Museum.)

Phillip Haddad Sr. opened his first store, the Leader, Inc., in 1913 in a small building on Front Street near Bayou Patassat. During World War I, a building on the corner of Front and Robert Streets became available. He bought the one-time saloon and changed it into a clothing and shoe store. After 50 years in business and having just celebrated his 70th birthday, Haddad died on a trip to his homeland of Lebanon. In early 1960, the building was demolished. Posing for the picture are, from left to right, (first row) Phillip Jr., Nellie, and Nebeha (on tricycle); (second row) Violet (leaning on the post), Phillip Sr., Janie (holding baby Liz); and Adele. The child riding the tricycle to the left is unidentified.

The icehouse on Front Street changed company names. Starting out in early 1900s as Slidell Ice & Electric, it then became Louisiana Public Utility Division of Associated Gas & Electric, then Gulf Public Service, and finally, Central Louisiana Electric Company in 1952. Ice was the company's main source of income until the 1950s. Electricity was supplied to the town's 1,714 customers in 1947, produced by the huge generators in the plant, as seen below. The average resident bought 25 to 50 pounds of ice every two days. The town's businesses and three dairies kept the company going. Ice prices were as follows: 5¢ for a half-pound block, 10¢ for 25 pounds, 20¢ for 50 pounds, and 50¢ for 100 pounds. The biggest customer was the White Kitchen. (Both, courtesy of Slidell Museum.)

Slidell Bargain House was one of the many small, independently owned businesses in Olde Town. This building was on the site of the present-day telephone company's central station, situated on the corner of Carey and Cousin Streets. (Courtesy of Slidell Museum.)

Then town's first newspaper was the *Bugle*, published in 1892, followed by the *Slidell Item* in 1897 and the *Slidell Brick* in 1899, which was edited by elementary school principal E.B. Shanks. The *Slidell Weekly News* began publishing in 1903 and was owned and operated by Marshall Thompson. He worked out of a building owned by P.E. Sarraille Sr. (Courtesy of Slidell Museum.)

Men working on the railroad and in shipyards patronized this Ballard parlor to pass the time. It was located on the corner of Erlanger and First Streets. The sign appears to read "Pastime Ballard Parlor." (Courtesy of Slidell Museum.)

Bowden opened the Barbecue Kitchen on Front and Erlanger Streets in 1900. Curb service was available for customers' convenience. When the White Kitchen opened, Mrs. Bowden (first name unknown) let its proprietors use her husband's sauce recipe for their famous barbecue dishes. It is not known if she sold the secret recipe or not. The town's water tower can be seen in this photograph. (Courtesy of Slidell Museum.)

In the early 1920s, Slidell's population was on the rise. Homes were under construction for workers and families, and the demand for home furnishings saw the introduction of furniture stores. These stores offered items manufactured in Slidell and those made elsewhere and delivered by rail. E.J. Pichon's Furniture Moving & General Hauling, pictured left, was located on Front Street. The site today is home to Levy's Furniture Store. Visible in the photograph are the city's water tower and the steeple of Our Lady of Lourdes Catholic Church, both located on First Street. Next to Pichon's is one of the town's many saloons. In the below photograph is Farr Furniture Company at an unknown location. The Farr family stands in front of the business. (Both, courtesy of Slidell Museum.)

Spanish Garden, later known as the Davis Inn, was located on Front Street between Teddy and Fremaux Avenues, across from the present train depot. Josephine Jahraus originally opened a small sandwich shop on the corner of Teddy Avenue. She then built a two-story, framed building in the middle of the block. The structure was completed on November 11, 1918. The sign in this photograph lists the establishment's offerings. Jahraus poses here with her niece. (Courtesy of GOSH.)

The Arcade Theatre was built in 1930 on Carey Street at a site where small-framed houses once stood. It first opened as a movie house with a stage. It hosted beauty and baby contests, magic shows, and other family events. Admission was 25¢, and a bag of popcorn and a Coke cost 5¢ each. In later years, the Deluxe Theater opened in the old Commissary Building on Front and Cleveland Streets. (Courtesy of GOSH.)

The first banking institution in town was Covington Bank & Trust Company. In 1906, the local branch broke from its parent company and formed Bank of Slidell on January 4 of that year. The bank was located on the corner of Front and Cousins Streets. Fritz and Albert Salmen, the town's largest industrial business employers, spearheaded the organization of the bank. The Bank of Slidell is on the left in this photograph. It was one of the first brick buildings in town. Slidell Masonic Lodge 311 (right) was established in 1906. The cornerstone of the building, located on Front Street, was laid on April 12, 1924. The Masons held their first meeting on April 7, 1906, and received three petitions. Between August and November 1906, twelve brothers were named Master Mason. (Courtesy of GOSH.)

The Slidell Savings & Homestead Association was located in the Carollo Building on Cousin Street in the 1920s. The float seen here, parked in front of Slidell High School on Third Street, was decorated for a parade commemorating the opening in 1928 of the Watson-Williams Bridge across Lake Pontchartrain. (Courtesy of GOSH.)

Here, two unidentified men and a small child stand in front of a five-and-ten store on Front Street between Bouscaren and Erlanger Streets. Early Slidell was a great place for small businesses to get started. As the town grew, so did the needs of the community. (Courtesy of Slidell Museum.)

Crescent Drug Company was owned by Dr. Joseph Feaston Polk, a surgeon, and Joseph Calvin Langston, s pharmacist. Their prescription department was open 24 hours a day. The store had the only soda fountain in town, and it was a great place for youngsters to visit. Dr. Polk (fifth from left) poses with an unidentified gentleman and children. (Courtesy of Slidell Museum.)

The Polk building was erected in 1911 in the heart of Olde Towne, standing on the corner of Cousin and Carey Streets. Dr. Polk, the first physician in town, was a prominent member of the community. The top floor of this building was leased to the telephone company. A 20-by-40-foot space in the rear was rented to the post office, and another space was a barbershop run by the Pravata family. (Courtesy of Slidell Museum.)

After Frank Cusimano graduated from Loyola's School of Pharmacy in the 1930s, he moved to Slidell, married, and opened his own business. Cusimano's Pharmacy was first opened at 202 Fremaux Avenue, as seen above, in early 1940. In the late 1940s, he moved the business to Front Street, pictured right, across from the train depot. This is the location most residents remember. Cusimano successfully ran for mayor of the town in 1962. That same year, Gov. Jimmy Davis declared the town a city. Cusimano could always be found at the drugstore, filling prescriptions and answering city-related questions. He held public office for 16 years. (Both, courtesy of Slidell Museum.)

Steve Haas is seen here walking near the Haas 5 and 10 Cents Store, a variety store on Cousin Street between Carey and First Streets. The business, started by his father, later moved to the newly constructed Tammany Mall Shopping Center on Pontchartrain Drive. It was renamed Haas' Ben Franklin 5 and 10. In the background of this photograph are signs for George's Hotel and Jitney Jungle. (Courtesy of Slidell Museum.)

James Champagne established Champagne's Department Store on Carey Street between Robert and Cousin Streets in 1920. It carried a wide variety of clothing, hardware, appliances, and home furnishings. It was one of many stores built with glass blocks for purposes of lighting and decor. (Courtesy of Slidell Museum.)

Slidell Cleaning and Pressing Shop, as listed in the 1935 telephone directory, was established in 1929. It moved from its previous location in 1939 to the corner of Robert and First Streets. The shop was owned and operated by Joe Johnson, one of the town's business leaders. A member of the Slidell Lion's Club, he was honored as King Samaritan in 1958 by the Slidell Women's Civic Club. Standing in front of the store in the photograph to the right are Joe Johnson, his wife Rhoda, and their son Bernard. In the below photograph, Joe Johnson (left) and an unidentified gentleman stand next to the pressing and dry-cleaning machine, still used until 1998. (Both, courtesy of Eric and Mary Dubuisson.)

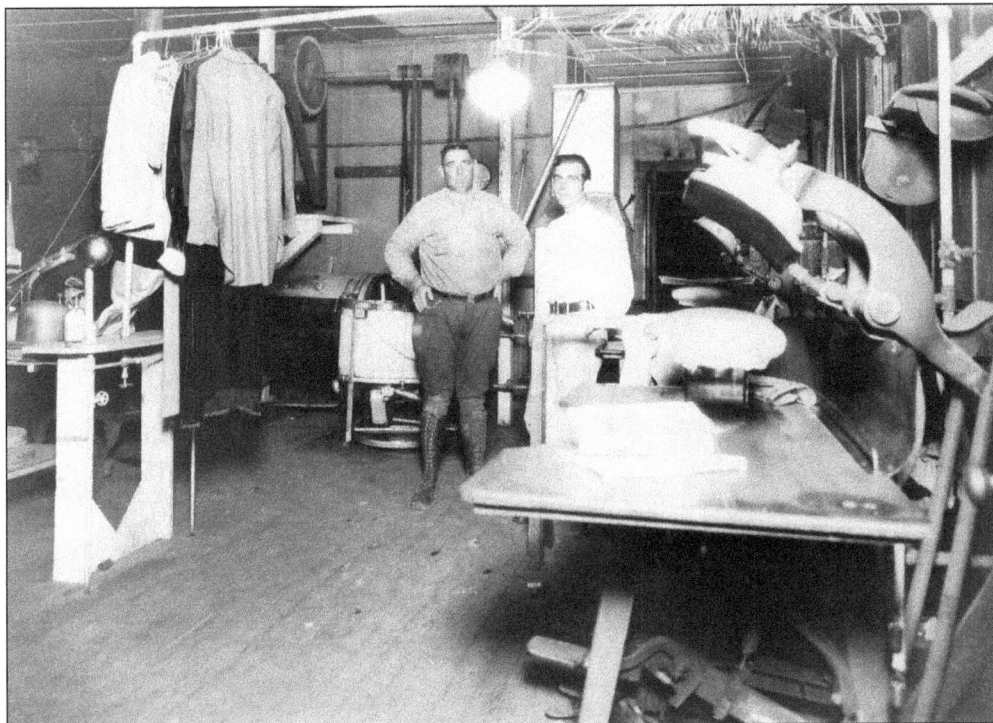

Sarraille's Market and Grocery, opened in 1940, was operated by P.E. Sarraille Sr. on Front Street, as seen above. Very few grocery stores were in Slidell at that time. His business specialized in fresh meat, poultry, and grocery products. In 1950, he tore the old store down and built a new one in the same location, pictured below. The author's memory of the store is of Andre, P.E.'s son, behind the counter with that huge smile. Andre served as a Slidell city councilman for many years. (Both, courtesy of Slidell Museum.)

Triangle Service Station, shown above in 1927, was located on Front Street. The gasoline and garage business started with two gas pumps under an oak tree. The company added more pumps and a canopy for protection from inclement weather. Owned by the Pravata family, the service station employed a number of town boys to offer day and night services. After World War I, the Pravatas bought more lots in the block, located across from the train depot, and it came to be known as "Triangle Square." The Pravatas added to the already thriving business a car dealership, as well as sales and service, seen below. (Above, courtesy of Slidell Museum; below, courtesy of GOSH.)

Langston's Rexall Drug Store on Front Street was established in 1929. It was run by Joseph Calvin Langston Sr. until 1941, when his son J.C. Jr. took over operations. It was famous for its soda fountain. Some of the town's leading citizens worked for the Langstons, including the following: Gus Fritchie (city judge), Jerry Hinton (senator), John Ray Swenson (longtime captain of Krewe of Perseus), Louise Innerarity, Marie Pichon, and Jack, Claude, and Mack Wolcott. In the early years, on a Saturday, folks would meet at the shop, get a soda, and sit on the porch and visit with neighbors and friends. In 1981, the building was torn down, and the land was leased to First Bank as a parking lot. (Both, courtesy of Slidell Museum.)

J.A. Mire opened his general store in 1916 on the corner of Robert and Carey Streets. Once Sabrier's pavilion and health resort, it was converted into J.A. Mire Hardware & Houseware. The family's living quarters were upstairs. In later years, J.A. remodeled the store, moving the entrance to the side on Carey Street. Mire's was one of the many businesses that survived the changing times, until Mrs. Mire (first name unknown) sold it in 1986. Shown in the above photograph are John "Shine" Mire, wearing a white apron, and three unidentified employees. Below, Mire's building is to the right, and to the left is the location of what was once Carollo Grocery Store. (Above, courtesy of Jan Mire Felder; below, courtesy of Slidell Museum.)

Porche's Conoco Station was located on the corner of Front Street and Liddle Avenue (presently Pontchartrain Drive). When the highway department decided to widen Highway 11, this service station was demolished and a new one built 12 feet back. It was replaced with a new station at the same location, and it remains today. (Courtesy of GOSH.)

Abney Service Station was built in 1927 by Walter L. Abney on Liddle Avenue (Pontchartrain Drive). The building was the home for many years of Sweeny's Plumbing Supply, run by Bob and Lynn Abney. A 1925 Ford can be seen parked on the side. (Courtesy of the Abney family.)

Ulysses Grant and Abner S. Neuhauser founded Neuhauser Bros. Ltd. in 1905. It became Neuhauser Incorporated in 1933. The original store was located on the west side of the railroad tracks. Mayor F.A. Bourgeois sold the brothers a 75-by-150-foot mercantile business across the tracks on Front Street. The Neuhausers carried everything from food to farm equipment. Their motto was "Every deal a square deal." The original store burned down and was replaced at the same location with this two-story building, located on the corner of Front Street and Fremaux Avenue. These unidentified ladies are going shopping at Neuhauser Bros. in the early 1920s. (Courtesy of Mildred Pearce.)

After spending a number of years learning the cleaning business from Joe Johnson of Slidell Cleaners, Samuel Emile Parks and his wife, Rosina, opened Modern Dry Cleaners in 1947. This is their building, on the corner of Front and Carey Streets. (Courtesy of Slidell Museum.)

The telephone company exchange opened in 1905 as Cumberland Telephone Company. It operated its 49 telephones from the entire second floor of the Polk Building. Southern Bell bought Cumberland properties in 1926. In 1960, the phone company served 3,845 customers. Some of those pictured in front of the exchange building are Verna ?, Maggie Fredrick, Ruby Davis, Earline Hinton, Euphan Whichard, and Midge Currie. A Mr. Hinyub stands the far left with a hat in hand. (Courtesy of Mildred Pearce.)

Andre J. Carollo's Grocery and Fruit Stand opened in the early 1920s. It was located on the corner of Robert and Carey Streets. The business was closed in 1965, and the site has been the location of a bicycle shop; currently, it is home to a restaurant. Standing in front of the store in the 1950s are Jimmy Carollo (left) and David Carollo. (Courtesy of Jan Mire Felder.)

Five

ABOUT THE COMMUNITY

Caring, giving, and a willingness to help one's fellow man—this should be the motto of Slidell's many clubs and civic organizations. Starting in early 1900 and through the years, the city's clubs have taken on many projects. The ladies of the town started the Pricilla Club in 1915. It began as a knitting club to send items overseas for the boys on the front lines and to loved ones far from home. After Greenwood Cemetery was donated to the city, the council voted to give the ladies all of the money generated from the cemetery for keeping up the grounds. Just like these ladies, Slidell Garden Club (established 1937) and Bayou Liberty Garden Club (established 1950) have taken on beautification projects for the city.

Slidell Lion's Club, established in 1928, was politically involved with the city; chartered members were doctors, lawyers, a mayor, aldermen, and businessmen—the backbone of the community. In the early years, these gentlemen erected street signs on corners and numbers on houses for the town's first home mail delivery.

Members of the Slidell Women's Civic Club (established 1947) were active in Mothers March of Dimes and the Girl Scouts, and they participated in door-to-door soliciting for the needy. They held the first Mardi Gras ball and parade to raise money for civic projects. Slidell Newcomer's Club (established 1962) helped the many families moving into the area in connection with the space program to interact socially and civically with the community.

The Slidell Junior Chamber of Commerce (established 1956) was organized to encourage young businesspeople between the ages of 21 and 35. It became inactive in late 1980. Established in 1962, the Slidell Chamber of Commerce has emerged as East St. Tammany Chamber of Commerce, promoting business and industry on the north shore. Slidell Rotary Club and Slidell Northshore Rotary host the Slidell Heritage Festival on the Fourth of July. The chapter of the Elks Lodge makes numerous trips to entertain the many senior caring centers in Slidell.

All of these organizations, along with others, help make Slidell a productive and caring community.

One of Slidell's oldest organizations, established on October 23, 1928, with 20 chartered members, is the Lion's Club. Its motto is "We Serve," and throughout the years, its members have done just that; not only for Slidell, but statewide. The fourth-oldest Lion's Club in Louisiana, it has been actively involved in many civic duties. In the above photograph, taken in 1951, Fulton Yates (left) and Joe Johnson stand with street signs for the city. They, along with other members, assembled and erected Slidell's first street signs for home mail delivery. Below, the Ladies Auxiliary sells refreshments at the dedication of Griffith Memorial Park on Second Street. Identified are, from left to right, Maggie Zinzer, "Grannie" Gayle, Cecile Hamelin, Lucy Mainegra, Laura McIntosch, and Laura "Babe" Champagne. (Both, courtesy of Slidell Lion's Club.)

The Priscilla Club began in November 1915 as a knitting club for the war effort, sending needed items to servicemen overseas. As years passed, the members extended their club duties by participating in civic-minded projects. In 1928, the ladies went before the mayor and city officials, seeking money to maintain Greenwood Cemetery. Elsie Salmen was the first president. Her family owned the cemetery property and would later donate it to the city. The ladies shown here are unidentified. (Courtesy of Slidell Museum.)

The Living Christmas Manger was started in 1954 by a group of individuals wanting to bring the holiday alive. Over 150 people participated in the pageantry from December 16 to Christmas Eve. From Christmas Day until New Year's Day, the live characters were replaced by figurines. The scene was located on the south end of Highway 11 (Pontchartrain Drive near Front Street). The event took place every year until early 1970. (Courtesy of Mildred Pearce.)

The Slidell Women's Civic Club started in 1947 with housewives and mothers joining together to help the city's' poor and needy. Even today, they are dedicated to the purpose of fostering civic, welfare, cultural, and the social interest in the community. One of their main fundraisers, begun in 1950, is the Carnival Ball. A king and queen are selected from individuals who have shown a deep commitment to their community. Maids and dukes are chosen from other organizations throughout the city. Even the men of the community participate in the ball. The 1952 presentation of the court is depicted in the above photograph. Shown are, from left to right, Olga Jennings, John Geiser, Hilda Wall, Lloyd Vivian, Eleanor McGinty, L.V. McGinty Sr., Billie Latulle, William Bulcao, an unidentified page, queen Grace Cusimano, king Robert Rugan Sr., three unidentified pages, Billie Sloat, Peter Carollo, Ruby Mayfield, Joseph Johnson, Helen Brock, A.J. Champagne, Glenn Brock, and Aline Vivian. The 1952 ball dancers in costume below are unidentified members. (Both, courtesy of Slidell Museum.)

The Ozone Camellia Club was formed on February 1, 1951. The object of the organization is to increase interest in camellias and to cultivate them. Slidell is called the "Camellia City," and a bloom is depicted on the city's flag. Through the efforts of Homer G. Fritchie, who was mayor, along with Ernest Judice and Joseph Johnson, the first meeting was held at the White Kitchen in Slidell. Twenty interested people attended that meeting. The first Camellia Show was held at the Slidell Motor Company. As many as 500 to 1,000 blooms were presented for judging. The winner of the grand prize in 1952 for his camellia, seen to the right, was Dr. James K. Howles of New Orleans. (Both, courtesy of Grace Fritchie Burkes.)

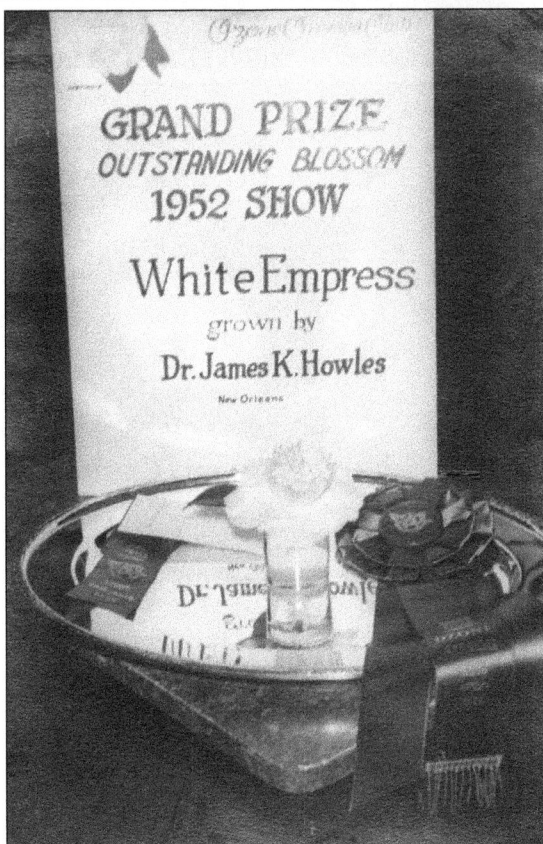

GRAND PRIZE
OUTSTANDING BLOSSOM
1952 SHOW
White Empress
grown by
Dr. James K. Howles
New Orleans

The first Ozone Camellia Court was presented in 1953, the club's second year. Pictured in the 1954 court are, from left to right, (seated) Margie Geiser and Queen Grace Fritchie Burkes; (standing) Judy Bulcao, Nancy Gayle, ? Plaunche, Joan Gardner, Diane Sloat, and Patsy Kennedy Folse. In 1955, boys were added as escorts. (Courtesy of Grace Fritchie Burkes.)

Many dignitaries over the years have had the honor of crowning the Queen of the Ozone Camellia Club. In 1954, Mississippi governor Hugh White (right) crowned Grace Fritchie Burkes. (Courtesy of Grace Fritchie Burkes.)

The first community school building was erected on College Street in the 1890s; it also served as a church. It was built by Rosa Salmen with donations from local residents. (Courtesy of GOSH.)

Salmen Park, seen here in the early 1940s, was located between First, Second, and Brakefield Streets. Through the efforts of many citizens and teams, an eight-foot fence and a grandstand were erected at the park. It was the home of many amateur athletes and teams, such as the Slidell Cardinals and a team for Harry Hoyle's Saloon. (Courtesy of Slidell Museum.)

Slidell's new era of entrepreneurs started with the formation of the Slidell Junior Chamber of Commerce (Jaycee/Jaynes) in 1956. These potential business leaders were between the ages of 21 and 35. Their goal was to teach and train entrepreneurs and encourage business growth in the town. Pictured above is the 1956 installation banquet of the Jaynes. Oscar Breeding is the master of ceremonies. The others are unidentified. After the junior chamber dissolved, a new group of businessmen formed the chamber of commerce in February 1962. Gus A. Fritchie Jr., Lionel G. Pichon, George A. Broom, Michael E. Haas, and W.T. Eddins were founding members. The 1917 building shown below was purchased and remodeled to meet the chamber's needs. It was once the home of the Charbonnet-Suarez family. (Above, courtesy of GOSH; below, courtesy of East St. Tammany Chamber of Commerce.)

Among the many festivals and outdoor events held in Slidell is the Heritage Festival, organized by the Rotary Club of Northshore and the Rotary Club of Slidell. The festival was started in 1998 as a way of raising money for local charities. Citizens of the community come together on July 4th every year to celebrate America's freedom and to support the community. (Courtesy of Lloyd Labatut.)

OLDE TOWNE

FIREWORKS   MUSIC   SOFT DRINKS   BOOTHS   ANTIQUES
CRAFTS   BEER   ARTS   GAMES

FIRST ANNUAL
SLIDELL
HERITAGE

JULY 4th
Festival '98

12 TILL 8:00 P.M.

Sponsored By
Slidell Picayune
Rotary Clubs of Slidell
City of Slidell

For Booth Information
Call 643-1234

POSTERS
DONATED BY

The Bayou Liberty Pirogue Races started in 1952. St. Genevieve Church was the initial sponsor. Later, residents of Bayou Liberty formed the Bayou Liberty Civic Club as a nonprofit organization to help children and the needy. The races were staged as a way to raise money for the club's projects. Pictured here are, from left to right, David Pichon, Bud Pichon, race founder Junior Pichon, and Troy Holden Sr. (Courtesy of the Pichon family.)

The pirogue races are held annually in June on Bayou Liberty on the St. Genevieve Church grounds. The races draw people from all over southeast Louisiana as spectators and contestants. This crowd is gathered at the old Galatas place, where some of the first races were held in early 1950. (Courtesy of the Pichon family.)

The Bayou Liberty Pirogue Races have a number of categories and age groups. Among the race categories are the common boat, the two-man canoe, and blindfold racing. In one race, rowers wear a paper bag over their head. Age categories include those over 40 and children from 8 to 12 and from 13 to 16. In this photograph, unidentified contestants head to the finish line. (Courtesy of the Pichon family.)

Community musicians played in parks and during outings. Today, the city still holds outdoor concerts for the public. Shown here is a group of unidentified players. (Courtesy of Slidell Museum.)

Slidell has many bayous and canals, where freshwater fishing, whether for pleasure or dinner, can easily be found. In the 1800s, seafood was one of the main exports to New Orleans. At far left in this photograph is "Mamma" Hilda Robinson Hambrick (1902–1984). At far right is Katie Elizabeth Hawkins, nicknamed "Grandma Kitty" (1847–1912). The others are unidentified. (Courtesy of Slidell Museum.)

After-school activities were a major part of growing up. These unidentified boys are taking advantage of some free time before afternoon chores. (Courtesy of Slidell Museum.)

Living and growing up on the bayou in Slidell is a way of life. These four unidentified teenagers pose on a ladder leaning against a railroad trestle crossing one of the area's many waterways. (Courtesy of Slidell Museum.)

The shores of Lake Pontchartrain are not far from the heart of the city. These unidentified ladies pose on a driftwood wharf. In the background, a lone camp juts out into the lake. (Courtesy of Slidell Museum.)

After church on Sunday, many families took advantage of the day with a leisurely stroll through the parks and trails along the bayou. This unknown group poses for a photograph. (Courtesy of Slidell Museum.)

Sailing on Bayou Bonfouca to Lake Pontchartrain was, and still is, a very scenic trip. These unidentified ladies are ready to sail the *Louisa*, built at one of the many shipyards in the area. (Courtesy of Slidell Museum.)

Family picnics and carriage rides through the many trails along the bayous was a pleasant outing. Today, Slidell has a number of parks for picnics and parties. These unidentified ladies and gentlemen enjoy an outing. (Courtesy of Slidell Museum.)

Six

SCHOOL, CHURCHES, AND CEMETERIES

Churches, houses of worship, and schools play an important part in any community's development. A number of early families in Slidell had an interest in education. The Linton family started one of the first private schools, in a backyard shed. The Salmens built a private school, which was also used as a church on Sunday. The first public school was located on Carey Street. After it burned down, a four-room building was erected on the corner of Carey and Brakefield Streets.

In 1910, Slidell built its first public school on that same corner, a three-story brick building accommodating grades one through eleven. In 1911, three hundred students were registered at what is now Brock Elementary. In 1908, Slidell High School was established, and around that same time, Mrs. U.G. Neuhauser started a Parent Teacher Association. In 1924, a new Slidell High was built on Third Street between Maine Street and Pennsylvania Avenue. The old high school became an elementary school. Changes through the years have brought Slidell from a frontier town to a community with high levels of education. Slidell's schools have come a long way, from a one-room shed to a state-of-the-art Salmen High School, which replaced the school destroyed by Hurricane Katrina in 2005.

In 1878, Starlight Missionary Baptist Church was built on the corner of Second and Erlanger Streets. It has been at this location since its establishment. By 1890, churches were being established all around town: Our Lady of Lourdes Catholic Church on First and Bouscaren Streets; First Community Church, built next to Salmen School House on College Street and used by Baptists under the ministry of C.D. Bowen; Methodist Church on Second and Guzman Streets, founded by a Mr. Kelly; and a Presbyterian Church established by J.M. Williams and used by the Episcopal congregation. In 1905, Mount Olive African Methodist Episcopal (AME) was built at 444 Guzman Street. First Presbyterian Church was built on Ninth Street.

As with life, there is death. In Slidell, two cemeteries were established. Land on Canulette Road was donated by the Guzman family for Our Lady of Lourdes Cemetery. In 1951, Salmen Brick & Lumber donated the property for Greenwood Cemetery on Second Street to the city.

Brother J.A.J. Kimp started Starlight Missionary Baptist Church in 1878. The church was named after it was formally established. The land on which the present church stands was purchased in 1891. The original church above was destroyed by fire in 1920. The congregation held services in a number of places until a new church was completed in 1921. Years later, the church was in need of renovation, so its congregation erected a smaller building on the side until a new one was built. On March 16, 1947, the cornerstone was laid for the new church. After 136 years, it remains in its original location on the corner of Second and Bouscaren Streets. (Above, courtesy of Starlight Missionary Baptist Church Ministry; below, courtesy of Bonnie Vanney.)

Christ Episcopal Church was founded in 1906. Carrie Comfort was the inspiration behind a petition filed for the church's recognition. James D. Grant, owner of Southern Creosoting Company, built a small green chapel on the corner of Fremaux Avenue and Third Street in 1922. Around 1955, the church moved to its present location on Seventh and Pennsylvania Streets. It was declared a parish in 1958. (Courtesy of Slidell Museum.)

A Methodist Mission was established in late 1890 by a circuit rider only known as Kelly. By 1895, members Horace Rousseaux and Gus McKinny had built this church north of what was Salmen Baseball Park, in the area of Brakefield, First, and Second Streets. (Courtesy of Slidell Museum.)

Rev. James Tucker organized First United Methodist Church on September 26, 1887. After services were held, 12 people professed their faith. The first church location was at Second and Guzman Streets. Behind the church was a graveyard, which is now part of Greenwood Cemetery. In 1905, the church moved to First Street between Robert and Cousin Streets, and in 1957, the congregation bought its present site on Third Street between Erlanger and Bouscaren Streets. (Courtesy of Slidell Museum.)

Mount Olive African Methodist Episcopal Church, located at 444 Guzman Street, is the oldest church building in Slidell. It was moved from the corner of First and Bouscaren Streets to its present location in the 1960s. It was originally Our Lady of Lourdes Church. (Courtesy of Bonnie Vanney.)

Evangelist John M. Williams established the First Presbyterian Church with three members on March 19, 1899. A newly constructed church was built on Ninth Street, and the doors were opened for worship in 1904. Women of the Church and Men of the Church are two active groups within the congregation. The church housed an Episcopal group for a number of years. (Courtesy of Slidell Museum.)

O.D. Bowen established the First Baptist Church on August 29, 1896. The first services for the church were held in Fritz and Rosa Salmen's home. Its first small wooden church was located on College Street. In 1910, the congregation moved to Carey and Robert Streets, shown here, on land donated by the Neuhauser family. Rosa Salmen once again helped the church by donating land for its present church on Pontchartrain Drive. (Courtesy of Slidell Museum.)

Slidell Baptist Church members board a flatbed car on Salmen Brick & Lumber's sidetrack, bound for Lacombe and Mandeville. Many parks were available in the area for outings. Salmen's brick kilns can be seen in this photograph. (Courtesy of Mildred Pearce.)

The cornerstone of Our Lady of Lourdes Church was set on September 14, 1890, on land granted to the archdiocese. A dedication mass took place on November 24, 1891, on the corner of First and Bouscaren Streets. The 1915 hurricane destroyed the church. A new church, school, and convent were built on the same site. Visible in the background is the town hall and jail. (Courtesy of Slidell Museum.)

The Cousin family established itself as extensive landholders between Bonfouca and Mandeville. In 1852, Madame Anatole Cousin built a brick church for her family on the Cousin property in the Bayou Bonfouca settlement. She was the daughter of Genevieve Dubuisson and Francois Pichon. The church was placed under the invocation of St. Genevieve, in memory of her mother. (Courtesy of GOSH.)

Located on Canulette Road, Our Lady of Lourdes Cemetery was once part of the plantation home of the Guzman family. Guzman Cemetery was donated to the archdiocese in 1926. The earliest interment took place in 1841. The cemetery is used today by many of the town's older families. (Courtesy of Bonnie Vanney.)

Originally owned by Salmen Brick & Lumber Company, Greenwood Cemetery was donated to the town of Slidell on May 11, 1951. The cemetery's name likely came from the timbers harvested from the land. Green wood is timber that has been freshly cut for processing. The oldest known interment, in 1894, is of Lee Liddle Salmen, age four. (Courtesy of Bonnie Vanney.)

Poole's Funeral Home was built in 1904 as a magnificent residence for a prominent Slidell pharmacist. Old records show that at one time, a Dr. P.R. Outlaw owned the property. Between 1938 and 1982, G.F. Poole ran a funeral home at this location. Today, the property is vacant. (Courtesy of Slidell Museum.)

Our Lady of Lourdes School, located on Second Street near Bouscaren Street, was built in 1929. The outer structure remains, but the interior has changed to accommodate offices of the mayor of Slidell. The building has served as city hall since 1973. (Courtesy of GOSH.)

The small building on the right of this photograph was used as a public school until 1910. The first public school was occupied in the old Knights of Pythias Hall on Louisa Street (presently Carey Street). Grades one through six were offered. The three-story building next door was the new Slidell School, used until 1939. (Courtesy of GOSH.)

When victory was declared after World War I, parades were staged to celebrate that occasion all over the United States, and Slidell was no exception. Schools throughout the parish were invited to attend a celebration parade. The above photograph shows the Slidell High School Band. A Mr. Hooper (on the horse) was the director of the band at the time of this parade. The others are unidentified. Below, local grammar-school children parade down Front Street. (Above, courtesy of GOSH; below, courtesy of Mildred Pearce.)

Slidell's first motorized school bus was introduced in 1925. The people shown here are not identified. (Courtesy of Slidell Museum.)

Members of the 1905–1908 St. Tammany Parish School Board pose for a group portrait. Unfortunately, their respective places in the photograph are not known. Their names and wards, obtained from the school board office, are as follows: John Englehardt (Ward One), D.C. Wallis (Ward Two), J.S. Jones (Ward Three), P.H. Hansberough (Ward Four), W.H. Kahl (Ward Five), Robert C. Abney (Ward Six), Howard Pierce (Ward Seven), P.W. Schneider (Ward Eight), C.M. Liddle (Ward Nine), A.D. Crawford (at-large), W.G. Evans (superintendent, 1905–1909). (Courtesy of Slidell Museum.)

This 1945 Slidell High School postcard was mailed from Pearlington, Mississippi. The school, completed in 1924, stood on Third Street between Maine Street and Pennsylvania Avenue. (Courtesy of Slidell Museum.)

This is the 1946 Slidell High School basketball team. Shown here are, from left to right, (first row) manager Leroy Wactor, Jerry Hinton, F.M. Pearce, Hoover Garrett, Bill Folse, Marvin Cocran, and Whitney Mayfield; (second row) coach L.V. McGinty, Edwin Panks, Curtis Fairburn, Jack Wolcott, Gus Fritchie Jr., Leighton Hill, and A.J. Lanoux. (Courtesy of Slidell Museum.)

The Slidell High School football team of 1932 poses for a portrait. Shown from left to right are (first row) Robert Villarubia, Robert Abney, David Cooley, Dominic Bruno, Peter Carollo, and J.R. Foley; (second row) Joe Hays, Shelby Galloway, Robert Rugan, Henry Keller, L.V. Cooley, C.D. Yates, and manager John "Bootie" Badon; (third row) Jack Taylor, Ralph Madison, coach L.V. McGinty, Andrew Crow, and Buster Baker. (Courtesy of Slidell Museum.)

Slidell High School won the 1945 football state championship. Posing here are, from left to right, (first row) coach L.V. McGinty, L.V. McGinty Jr., Jack Wolcott, Cut Nunez, Sidney Hursey, Gus Fritchie, Jack Gomez, Tom Abney, Bill Folse, and manager Leonard Horsey; (second row) Edwin Panks, Leonard Seller, Jimmie Johnson, John Holdsworth, Perry Whitfield, F.M. Pearce, Curtis Fairburn, Bernard Betram, and manager Gerry Hinton; (third row) Earl Broom, Warren Allen, Leighton Hill, Marvin Cocran, Hoover Garrett, Joe Baragona, and Eddie Mayfield; (fourth row) John Nix, Jerry Whitfield, E.B. Parker, J.C. Naulty, Leroy Wactor, Donald Anglin, and Kermit Holden; (fifth row) Emile Sarraille, Joe Todd, Jennie Hover, Thomas Whichard, and Chuck Evans. (Courtesy of Slidell Museum.)

Until 1965, there were two Catholic churches in the Slidell area: St. Genevieve in the Bayou Bonfouca settlement and Our Lady of Lourdes in Olde Towne. Honoring Mary, Mother of God during May brings many festivals and adorations. Crowning the Blessed Mother during May can be a daily or weekly celebration. It is a special honor to be chosen as the one who crowns her and as one of the maids who are picked for the ceremony. The photograph to the left was taken in 1948 at the shrine of Our Lady on the school grounds. The Maids of the May are unidentified. Shown below is the 1936 May Festival of Our Lady of Lourdes Church. King Leroy Broom sits on the left and queen Anne Mire is on the right. The pages are unidentified. (Left, courtesy of GOSH; below, courtesy of Slidell Museum.)

Seven

PEOPLE WHO MADE A DIFFERENCE

There are names of people in a community that should be remembered as significant contributors to its growth and development, and the outstanding residents of Slidell are no exception. Financier Baron Fredric Emile von d' Erlanger brought the railroad through the town and named it Slidell after his father-in-law, John Slidell. John Evariste Guzman was a major landowner whose tract 44 became part of Slidell. Pierre Thomas Robert and his son Iunot Angelo Robert owned land surrounding Robert's Landing. In the late 1800s, this was the heart of town. Today, it is Heritage Park. George Gause, Oscar R. Brugier, and Armand Cousin held substantial parcels that later developed into commercial, as well as residential, subdivisions.

Most of the street names in the city reflect people and families who surveyed land and settled here. Leon J. Fremaux and G. Bouscaren, both engineers and surveyors for the railroad, mapped out the town. J.E. Brakefield was an independent surveyor. Carey Street was named for John Guzman's wife, Mary Ann Cary.

Fritz and Albert Salmen were the owners of Salmen Brick & Lumber Company. The Schneider family currently owns St. Joe Brick Works, purchased in 1891. Andrew D. Canulette was one of the principal owners of the Slidell Shipbuilding Company, which was later renamed Canulette Shipyard.

Dr. John Keller Griffith started practicing medicine in town around 1911. He was elected to the US House of Representatives in 1936 as a first-time politician. Griffith Park in central Slidell is named in his honor. Dr. Joseph Feaston Polk made house calls on horseback until Slidell grew enough for roads to be built. He then used a horse and buggy and, later, a Model T Ford.

These are only a few of the many people who have played a part in Slidell's history.

John Slidell Jr. was born in 1793, the first of four children to John Slidell Sr. and Margery Mackenzie of New York. Educated in New York and, later, Louisiana, he studied law and became a successful merchant, lawyer, politician, and staunch defender of Southern rights as a US representative and US senator for Louisiana. Pres. Jefferson Davis appointed him as special Confederate envoy to France in 1861. His mission was to help preserve the Confederacy by negotiating an alliance with Britain, seeking diplomatic assistance and procuring war resources. While waiting to board an English ship at Boston Harbor, he and his wife were arrested and deported to France. As Slidell was a Confederate official, neither he nor his wife was allowed to return to the United States after the Civil War. In 1883, after the completion of the railroad line from New Orleans, the first stop crossing Lake Pontchartrain was named in his honor. He died in 1871, before the station was named Slidell. (Courtesy of GOSH.)

While attending a private school in New York, Marie Mathilde Deslonde Slidell became friends with John Slidell's sister, Jane. And it was there that she met John. She was born to one of the wealthiest and grandest plantation owners in Belle Point, St. John the Baptist Parish, Louisiana. Marie Mathilde Deslonde married John in 1835. They had a large family; only four of the children survived to accompany them to France. The others are buried in the family tomb in Reserve, Louisiana. (Courtesy of GOSH.)

Marguerite Mathilde Slidell was the daughter of John and Mathilde Slidell. While in Paris, the family was treated with great respect. In Biarritz, Marguerite and her mother attended a reception and were graciously received by Emperor Napoleon III. She met and married Baron Fredric Emile von d'Erlanger, one of the financers of the railroad. He named the town Slidell in honor of his father-in-law. (Courtesy of GOSH.)

The John Guzman family is pictured about 1902. Identified from left to right are (first row) Ella Guzman (7 years old), Midge Currie, (8) Beanie Levy (8), Florence Guzman (5), Gertrude Levy (3), Sam Currie (5), Jimmy Levy (5), Ana Maria Cooper Cary (seated), Charles Guzman (3), Geneva Whichard (3), Tommy Whichard (4), and Jimmy Currie (3); (second row) Caro Levy or Pearl Currie, Sweetie Levy (10), Molly Guzman (8), Rora Whichard (6), Forest Whichard

(8), Henry "Red" Currie (10), and Arthur Whichard (7); (third row) Nannie Levy (39 years old, holding Burnette), Jim Currie, Charles Guzman, Mamie Currie (37, holding Laura, 1), Sally W. Guzman (wife of Charles Guzman, holding Amelia, 2), John E. Guzman (74), Noemie Whichard (29, holding Euphan, 1), Sam Levy, 18), Bonaparte Theodore Faciane (24), Joseph E. Faciane (22), Henry Levy (16), and Annie Levy (14).

Among the early and oldest settlers in Slidell and the Bonfouca area was the Guzman family. John Guzman Sr. was born in 1795 and died in Slidell in 1858. He inherited his vast land holdings from Bartholemy Martin. The property consisted of the south part of Slidell, including Eden Isles. By an act of Congress, track 44 was approved on April 20, 1854. It contained 5,000 acres. As a businessman, Guzman owned a sawmill, brickyard, hospital, ferry, and general store. The family's plantation home was located on a parcel of land off Canulette Road, near Our Lady of Lourdes Cemetery (Guzman Cemetery). John Jr. followed his father into the family businesses. John married Mary Ann Cary on December 28, 1857, at Annunciation Church in New Orleans. They settled on the bayou and had ten children, with seven living to become adults. John died on December 12, 1914, and is buried in the family tomb. (Courtesy of Mildred Pearce.)

John Fritz Salmen (who went by "Fritz") and Rosa Liddle married in 1882. They moved to Slidell from Handsboro, Mississippi, in 1883 or 1884. At about age of 23, John began developing new ideas for brick making and lumber production, using what he learned from his uncle Henry Linehard. After settling in Slidell, he purchased his first tract of land, east of the railroad line, in 1884. Salmen's land extended from Bayou Patassat south to Bilten Street, and from the railroad line east to a point between College and Louisa (presently Carey) Streets. His business holdings included a lumberyard, brickyard, and a shipyard, where he built schooners for transporting his products. In 1910, the company employed 800 people. Salmen's company built housing for its employees and started a school and a church. People called this section of town Salmentown. He was one of the town's first aldermen and was president of the Bank of Slidell. (Courtesy of GOSH.)

The youngest son of Catherine and John Salmen, Albert joined his brother Fritz and later Jacob in the lumber and brick business. Having lost their father in 1867, Albert, like his brother, was taught the business by their uncle. When Albert and Elsie Sollberger moved to Slidell, they built a large house in Salmentown, seen below. Not to be outdone by his brother, Fritz built a beautiful cypress mansion on the corner of Cleveland Avenue and Front Street. It was completed in 1895. They had no children when Elsie's sister Louisa lost her husband, Gustav Fritchie, in 1908. She had no means of support, so Albert and Elsie took them in and raised the four boys, who became an important part in Slidell's history. Homer was mayor of Slidell from 1930 to 1962, Gus Sr. became Slidell's first city court judge, Charles J. Fritchie Jr. was a historian for Guardians of Slidell History, and Albert worked in the family business. (Above, courtesy of GOSH; below, courtesy of the Homer G. Fritchie family.)

Ulysses Grant and Abner S. Neuhauser came to Slidell because of the railroad. Grant was a station agent for 13 years and a large holder of town and country real estate. He took an active interest in the town's education. Neuhauser was the manager of Slidell Brick Works until it closed. Around this time, they opened the mercantile business. Shown here is the Neuhauser family. The identities of the individual members are not known. (Courtesy of Slidell Museum.)

T.J. Eddins held an important position in the Salmen Brick & Lumber Company. He formed a copartnership with C.A. Everett to sell real estate in the city and in the rural area of St. Tammany Parish. Their office was inside the Bank of Slidell building on Front Street. The Bank of Slidell members shown here are, from left to right, Grant Neuhauser, Harry Peterson, a Mr. Hailey, and T.J. Eddins, president. (Courtesy of Mildred Pearce.)

Dr. Joseph Feaston Polk was the equivalent of the Old West frontier doctor, first making house calls and answering emergencies on horseback. As time progressed and roads were built, he used a horse and buggy. After serving a tour of duty in World War I, Polk returned to Slidell and used a more modern form of transportation, a Model T Ford. After graduating from the University of Tennessee Medical School in 1898, he hung his shingle in Slidell during the winter of that same year. With his wife of seven years, Marganie Elizabeth Langston Polk, a schoolteacher, they began a long and productive life in a small railroad community. Above, Dr. Polk is seen in front of his office. The photograph to the left shows his "lighter side," according to a note on the back of the image. (Both, courtesy of Slidell Museum.)

In the photograph to the right, taken in the mid-1900s, Dr. Polk sits in front of the building in Olde Towne. Marganie Polk began teaching Sunday school and grade school when she first arrived in town. She and Dr. Polk were on the building committees of the high school, grammar school, and original First Baptist Church. In 1950, Mayor Homer Fritchie declared a "Dr. Polk Day," highlighted by a parade of all the adults, teenagers, children, and babies that he had brought into the world. The fine house that he and Mrs. Polk built, pictured below, is located on the corner of First and Bouscaren Streets. Polk continued to make house calls until 1958, when he was found dead behind the wheel of his car in front of his house. (Right, courtesy of GOSH; below, courtesy of Slidell Museum.)

E.J. Perilloux and J.D. Kitchen established Slidell Brick & Tile Company to compete with Salmen Brick & Lumber Company. In the early development of Slidell, there was a rivalry between uptown and downtown. Slidell Brick & Tile was located near the site of today's Northside Mall, off West Hall Avenue. Salmen was located at the south end of town. (Courtesy of Slidell Museum.)

Napoleon "Leon" Joseph Fremaux was born in New Orleans. He was the oldest son of Francois Etienne Fremaux. When he was old enough, his parents sent him to the College Louis Le Grand in Paris, France, to study engineering. He returned to New Orleans to practice his skills. In 1855, he was appointed state engineer. Fremaux was a surveyor, engineer, architect, and an accomplished artist. He served in the Louisiana National Guard as a lieutenant colonel in 1880. He was one of the surveyors that laid out the town of Slidell in 1882. (Courtesy of Slidell Museum.)

112

Oscar R. Brugier built this magnificent two-story home in Slidell on square eight, which is now known as Brugier Subdivision. It was situated between First and Second Streets and Pennsylvania Avenue and Michigan Street. He established an experimental farm, which tapped the undeveloped resources of the area. Slidell was so involved with the logging and lumber business, it neglected its natural resources. On this site, Brugier showed his friends and neighbors how to increase the production of certain crops. Growing cotton via an intelligent method of cultivation could produce one bale per acre. The development of sugarcane was equally promising, including the production of a richer saccharine content than that grown in other regions. Other vegetables and fruits, such as strawberries and sweet potatoes, could yield double the amount. The soil and climate were favorable not only for produce, but for all kinds of livestock. (Courtesy of Slidell Museum.)

1925--STATE OF LOUISIANA

This is to Certify

That MRS. JOSEPHINE E. BRUGIER

a Licensed Real Estate Broker, whose address is

New Orleans & Slidell, La., has been issued

License No. 2500-2486 as a **Real Estate Broker,** until

December 31, 1925

LOUISIANA REAL ESTATE BOARD
Association of Commerce Building,
New Orleans, La.

Josephine Batts Radditich Brugier Jahraus's long history began in 1909, when she married her first husband, a Mr. Radditich. They left New Orleans and moved to Slidell due to his health. Having learned the millinery business at a very young age, she opened a small store in conjunction with her dressmaking, located on the corner of Robert and Carey Streets. Her first foray into real estate was the purchase of a house on Bayou Liberty. The piney woods were better suited for her husband's condition. Unfortunately, the sale fell through, and they moved back into town. The Carollo family had a small store with living quarters in the rear that she rented, and she opened another millinery, dressmaking, and notions store. She and her husband opened a picture show in the Community House on Robert Street. Josephine later purchased a two-story house on Robert Street and opened a millenary shop with a boardinghouse upstairs. Across the street, they leased a lot from the Bank of Slidell and opened the Airdome, an open-air picture show. After her husband's passing, she married Oscar R. Brugier. With that marriage, she acquired her vast land holdings. She donated the land for Slidell Hospital. (Courtesy of Slidell Museum.)

Dr. John Keller Griffith came to Slidell around 1911. He married Vivian Comfort, a local girl, and they raised two children. Griffith Park was named for the longtime physician. On his first bid for public office, Griffith was elected in 1936 to represent Louisiana's Sixth Congressional District. With his election, it was the first and only time the area elected someone to the US House of Representatives. Slidell is now in the First Congressional District. The city erected a monument to Griffith, originally at the triangle formed by First and Front Streets. It was later moved to the park next to the City Auditorium, located on Second Street. The park hosts many events, including Christmas Under the Stars, concerts in the park, and the Camellia Market. (Courtesy of Bonnie Vanney.)

After the resignation of Mayor Alonzo Badon due to the town's bad economic conditions, Homer G. Fritchie was elected the 16th mayor of Slidell in 1930. He remained in office until 1962. As a businessman with administrative skills, he was able to turn the town's economy around. His great love for the community and its citizens was overwhelming. The year he took office, Slidell's population was 2,807, the Rigolets Bridge had just opened as a free bridge to Slidell, the council changed the city charter to a four-year term, Robert Mayfield was appointed the first policeman, and J.E. Decker was named fire chief. Through the Depression, the city faced a $40,000 debt, but through the efforts of the city council and the Bank of Slidell, it managed to stabilize the economy. Another major accomplishment during his administration was passing an ordinance for subdivision regulations and rules for infrastructure. Mayor Fritchie died on September 22, 1977, at age 82. (Courtesy of Slidell Museum.)

Homer Fritchie's office building was located in the northeast corner of Cleveland and William Tell Streets. From this small office, he ran a profitable engineering company. His signature can be seen on many city maps and surveys. (Courtesy of Slidell Museum.)

The 1963 Camellia Show chairman was the newly retired mayor Homer Fritchie. Here, he is seen holding the ribbon and flower for best bloom grown in the open, achieved by Jane Moon of Lake Charles, Louisiana. (Courtesy of Grace Fritchie Burk.)

Charles F. McMahon, mayor from 1892 to 1894, was not as colorful as some other Slidell mayors. McMahon was one of the original aldermen who drafted and signed Slidell's first charter in 1888. His election resulted in a tie. The city charter called for a vote of the council, and McMahon was unanimously elected. (Courtesy of Slidell Museum.)

Paul J. Gardere was the ninth mayor of Slidell (1910–1914). When he took office, the population was 2,188. Slidell had eight saloons, and a franchise was granted to Cumberland Telephone Company. The town purchased its first road machine. During Gardere's term, the town began lighting the streets, and a new, larger depot replaced the old one. (Courtesy of Slidell Museum.)

Andrew D. Canulette served as mayor from 1924 to 1928. He was also one of the principal owners of the Slidell Shipbuilding Company. The family would later become principal owners in Canulette Shipbuilding. During his term in office, a franchise was granted for the construction of the Watson-Williams Bridge (Five-Mile Bridge), the new high school was built on Third Street between Maine and Pennsylvania Streets, and the city purchased its first fire engine. (Courtesy of Slidell Museum.)

Alonzo L. Badon was twice elected mayor. He served from 1916 to 1920 and from 1928 to 1930. During his first term, the city was still enjoying the economic profits of its industries. Shipbuilding was at an all-time high, with large oceangoing vessels being launched daily. Tourism was becoming Slidell's newest industry. During his second term in office, Badon dealt with the depressed economy due to the war. He resigned during his second year in office. (Courtesy of GOSH.)

SLIDELL, LOUISIANA
SLIDELL, LOUISIANA

In this 1925 photograph, Carroll C. Pravata, brother of Pete D. Pravata, longtime political and civic leader, sits at the wheel of an American Lafrance fire truck. Standing in front is Frank Carroll. They are parked on the side of Triangle Garage, which was located at First and Front Streets. (Courtesy of Slidell Museum.)

Pravata Airpark was located between US Route 190 and West Hall Avenue, in what are now Carolyn Park and Hermandel Subdivisions. The Civil Air Patrol was organized in May 1944. Slidell Flight elected officers on May 11, 1944, under the guidance of a flight lieutenant from New Orleans and Lieutenant Morrill of Slidell. Slidell Flight "E" civil Air Patrol had 22 men and a Cadet Army Auxiliary made up of boys under the age of 18. In 1951, the 39th Infantry Division, Aviation Section Unit of the Louisiana National Guard used Pravata Airpark for drills. These unidentified men are in a training session. (Courtesy of Slidell Museum.)

Eight

THE PRICE TO PAY

These last few pages are dedicated to reflecting on something that will forever be a part of our lives and history. The vintage photographs, wedding pictures, children's portraits, family albums that cannot be replaced are gone. That heirloom belonging to family members long gone was tossed on a pile in the front yard, destined for the dump. Hurricane Katrina is a part of history that will be thought about now and for generations to come.

It has been said after that Hurricane Katrina, anybody living in a state bordering the Gulf of Mexico is crazy. Mother Nature has proven that wrong by the weather phenomena that have occurred since Katrina. Residents of Southeast Louisiana have come to adapt, just like people in other regions of the United States. People in northern and eastern states living on major tributaries or near the Atlantic Ocean face the same flooding and damaging winds. Folks here prefer to live in a hurricane-prone area than in Tornado Alley or to get blanketed by a snowstorm. Anywhere one lives, it is his or her home, and nobody wants to lose what they have worked so hard to attain. Louisiana has been recording major hurricanes and flooding since the 1800s. Orleans, St. Tammany, and other parishes bordering Lake Pontchartrain are subject to flooding from water pushed in from Lake Borgne and the Gulf of Mexico. Bayous that lead into Slidell off Lake Pontchartrain were her major ports during the industrial era. Now, they are scenic waterways with lovely homes dotting the bayou. When water rises in the lake, the bayous back up, causing flooding. The first recorded major flooding occurred in Slidell in 1881. It lasted eight days before the water receded.

Areas that flooded during Hurricane Katrina were not inhabited until the 1960s, so damage was minimal. Places remembered by residents when they were children have been torn down, not to be replaced. The neighborhoods are not the same. Many people have left, many never came back; new friends were made to replace the ones that are no longer here.

These are things that will be remembered not only by the residents of Slidell, but also by their children and grandchildren.

Seen here is Olde Towne on First Street. Floodwaters entered the town from the south. On the left, a small building over the top of a submerged vehicle and a white post in front can be seen. This is the location of the Slidell Museum, one of two buildings that housed many of the city's old records, documents, and photographs. Down the street on the right is a bank. Across the street is the Polk family home. (Courtesy of GOSH.)

Heritage Park is located on Bayou Bonfouca. In the early 1800s, when the railroad was being constructed, this area was considered the heart of town. Today, the park is used for festivals, concerts, and many other city events. There are boat launches and a dock area for fishermen. (Courtesy of St. Tammany Fire District No. 1.)

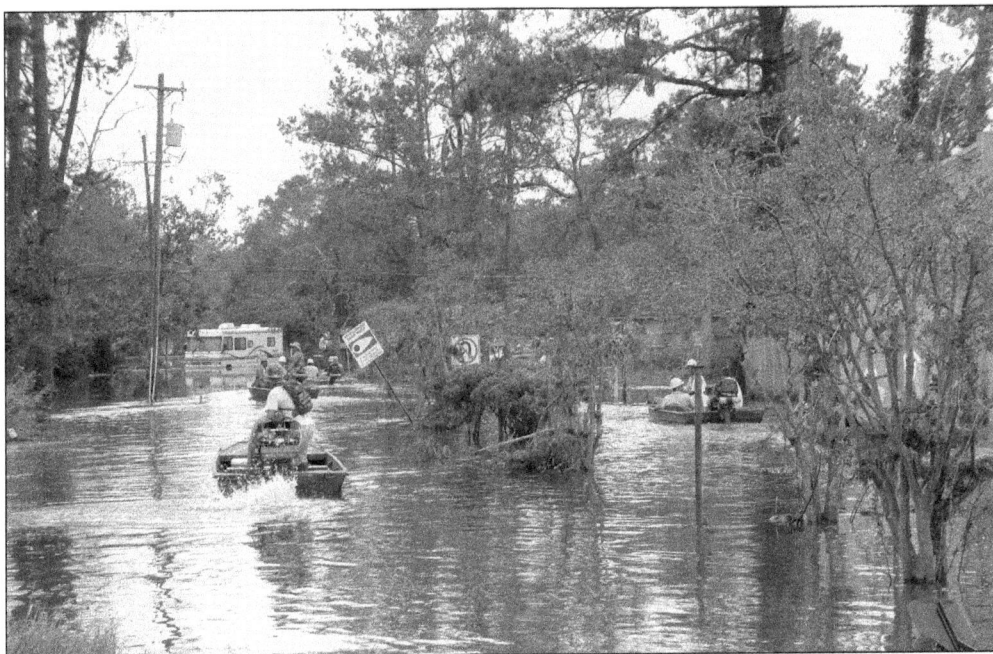

One of the hardest-hit areas after Hurricane Katrina's passing was south Slidell. Here, rescue workers are going into a subdivision, looking for residents who might have stayed behind. Water was as high as six to eight feet in homes. Some residents could not return for weeks after the storm to assess their damage. (Courtesy of St. Tammany Fire District No. 1.)

In the early 1800s, Fremaux Avenue and Front Street, across from the train depot, was the location of the Neuhauser Bros. store. On the left is that building without the second story, and on the right was where the Commercial Hotel stood. It is now a closed service station. Floodwaters were not as high in this area. Visible down Fremaux Avenue is a row of commercial buildings. (Courtesy of St. Tammany Fire District No. 1.)

Fritz Salmen built this beautiful cypress mansion in 1895 on the corner of Cleveland Avenue and Front Street. Hurricane Katrina did minor damage to the structure, but the beautiful oaks that dotted the property were destroyed. (Courtesy of St. Tammany Fire District No. 1.)

This photograph looks down Bouscaren Street from Front Street. In the rear, at center, the Slidell City Court building can be seen. On the left is Roberta Cleaners. It has seen many floodwaters since its construction in the early 1900s. On the right is the Gus Baldwin building, boarded up to protect it from high winds, but not from floodwaters. This photograph was taken a few days after Hurricane Katrina. (Courtesy of St. Tammany Fire District No. 1.)

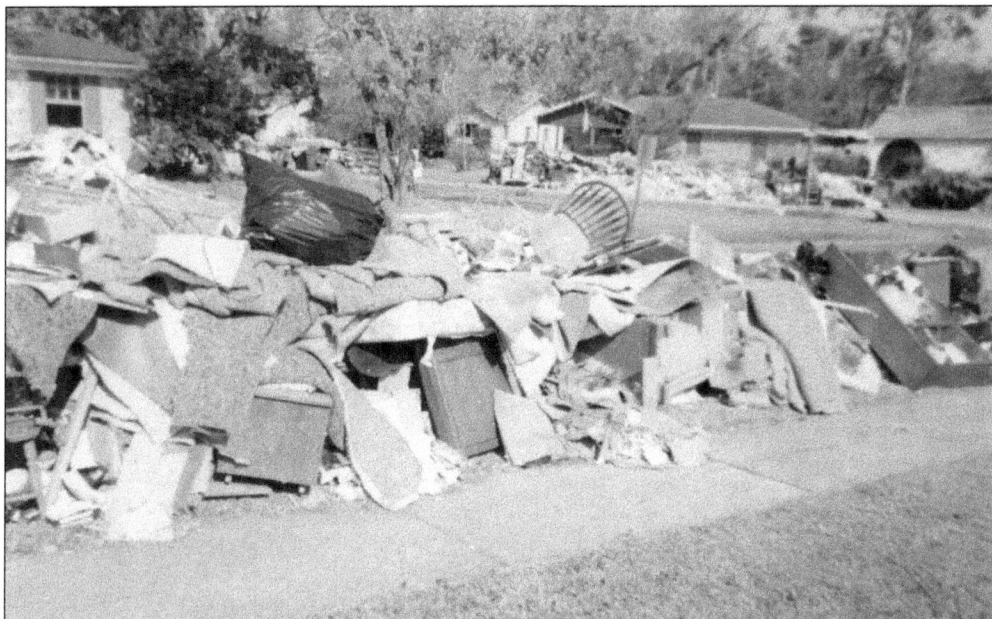

This photograph depicts the destruction that Katrina did on the south end of Slidell. This subdivision is located 2.9 miles from Lake Pontchartrain. There was six feet of water in homes in this area. The author knows these details firsthand, as she stayed and rode the storm out in a canoe for seven hours. This photograph was taken in front of the author's house and that of her neighbor's, two weeks later. (Courtesy of Bonnie Vanney.)

Damage in the city was nothing like what occurred on the shoreline of Lake Pontchartrain. A storm surge of 18 to 20 feet occurred along the lakeshore. Houses were reduced to rubble; boats from the marina were tossed around like toys in the Eden Isles community. (Courtesy of St. Tammany Fire District No. 1.)

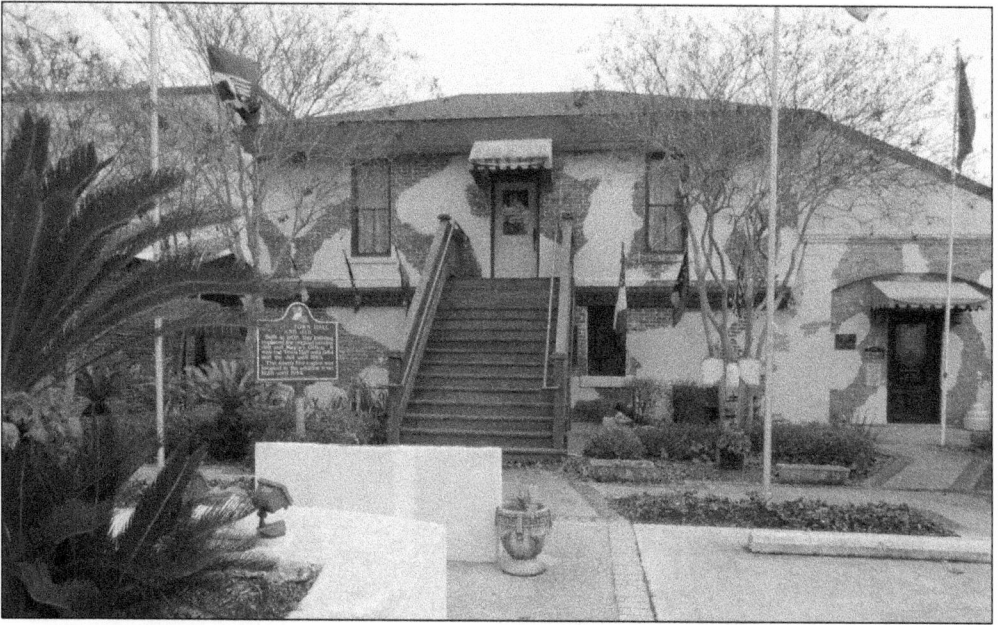

In 1888, City Hall was a small, two-room wooden building on First Street. One room was for the jail, and the other was the mayor's office. In 1907, the wooden building was moved, and a permanent brick building was constructed on the site. Upstairs was the mayor's office, and downstairs was the jail. In 1927, an addition was erected to the right of the building to house the city's fire engine. Today, it is the home of the Slidell Museum. (Courtesy of Bonnie Vanney.)

In 1973, the former Our Lady of Lourdes school building, located on Second Street, was transformed into the current City Hall. The outer structure is the original building. The interior was gutted to accommodate the city's needs. It has been renovated a number of times in the last 41 years. (Courtesy of Bonnie Vanney.)

BIBLIOGRAPHY

Ellis, Dan. Slidell "Camellia City," Pass Christian, Ms. Dan Ellis, 1999.
Fritchie Jr., Charles J. *Notes on Slidell History*. Slidell, LA: Guardians of Slidell History, 1999.
Vanney, Arriollia. *An Island Between the Chef and Rigolets*. Arriollia Vanney, 1998.
———. *The Lost and Forgotten Communities of Chef Menteur-Rigolets and Lake St. Catherine in Orleans Parish*. Arriollia Vanney, 2007.

Visit us at
arcadiapublishing.com

www.ingramcontent.com/pod-product-compliance
Lightning Source LLC
Chambersburg PA
CBHW050554110426
42813CB00008B/2355